"Leeana says out loud the things we all feel, and she says it with grace and eloquence. I'm so thankful for her honesty and her wisdom. Reading these pages is like sitting with a friend, and that's the best thing I can think of."

—Shauna Niequist,
author of *Bread & Wine*

"A new lyrical voice in a crowded world, Tankersley tells a tale of hope, reality, and everything in between."

—Claire Díaz-Ortiz,
author, speaker, and innovator at Twitter, Inc.

"In *Breathing Room*, Leeana Tankersley speaks the kind of soul language I'm always looking for but rarely find, the kind that comes from thoughtful silence, faithful waiting, and long, dark nights. She refuses to reach for easy answers, instead leading the reader on a journey of accepting our own humanity—to turn toward Christ and grieve fully, celebrate wildly, breathe deeply in his presence—and begin again. Quite simply, this is one of the most thoughtful books I've read all year."

—Emily P. Freeman,
author of *A Million Little Ways*

breathing
room

breathing room

letting go so you can fully live

LEEANA TANKERSLEY

Revell

a division of Baker Publishing Group
Grand Rapids, Michigan

Published by Revell
a division of Baker Publishing Group
P.O. Box 6287, Grand Rapids, MI 49516-6287
www.revellbooks.com

Printed in the United States of America

Library of Congress Cataloging-in-Publication Data is on file at the Library of Congress, Washington, DC.

ISBN 978-0-8007-2346-0

Scripture quotations marked Message are from *The Message* by Eugene H. Peterson, copyright © 1993, 1994, 1995, 2000, 2001, 2002. Used by permission of NavPress Publishing Group. All rights reserved.

Scripture quotations marked NIV are from the Holy Bible, New International Version®. NIV®. Copyright © 1973, 1978, 1984, 2011 by Biblica, Inc.™ Used by permission of Zondervan. All rights reserved worldwide. www.zondervan.com

The author is represented by Christopher Ferebee, Attorney and Literary Agent. www.christopherferebee.com

14 15 16 17 18 19 20   7 6 5 4 3 2 1

To Luke, Lane, and Elle with all my love

contents

prelude
breathing

But me he caught—reached all the way
    from sky to sea; he pulled me out
Of that ocean of hate, that enemy chaos,
    the void in which I was drowning.
They hit me when I was down,
    but God stuck by me.
He stood me up on a wide-open field;
    I stood there saved—surprised to be loved!

Psalm 18:16–19 Message

The human body's urge to breathe is irrepressible and essential. When we hold our breath, we begin to feel a pain inside our chest. This is called our critical line, a signal it's time for another breath. Everyone's critical line is different, but everyone—at some point—must breathe.

Research shows we hit our critical line, not necessarily because our body needs oxygen, but because our body needs to release CO_2. When we hold our breath, our body tells us it's time to exhale. Only then can we take in the air we need.

"As it turns out," a breathing researcher writes, "the opposite of holding your breath isn't inhaling, it's letting go."

Over the past four years of my life—which have included the birth of my first children (boy/girl twins), the challenges of learning to be a working writer, two moves within my hometown of San Diego, a miscarriage, another pregnancy, a move to the Middle East for my husband's job in the Navy, the birth of our third child in the Middle East, and a move back to San Diego with three small children in tow—I have been through a bit of a Come Apart. Or, to say it in breathing terms, I hit my critical line.

I had been holding my breath for years—probably more years than I realized—trying to manage the pain in my chest. Trying to stave off surrender. Trying to keep it all together.

Until I couldn't anymore.

This is not to say the last four years have been horrible. They haven't. In most every way, they have been the richest, most textured years we've lived.

Which is why things got so very confusing. If life was so beautiful (and it was) and I had so much to be grateful for (and I did), why was I struggling? Why did I feel like I was being squeezed relentlessly? Why did everything feel so urgent? So suffocating? All the time?

Sure, we had stress. No one would deny that. But our *life* wasn't coming apart, not in the ways you think of someone's life crumbling. If anything, our life was arriving, precious dose after precious dose.

Still, I could not breathe.

My inability to suck it up and manage exposed and high-lighted my growing suspicion that I was grossly inadequate for my own life. I begrudged my critical line and believed something was wrong with me because I couldn't just push past it like it seemed so many others were able to do, like I had always been able to do.

My refusal to exhale, to let go, just about drowned me.

I needed someone or something to release the valve on the blood pressure cuff that was squeezing my soul. I needed the anxious intensity to dissipate. I needed a place I could go where no one would try to convince me of how blessed I am or how I should simply pray harder. I needed people and words and spaces that were filled with grace, that honored my struggle. I needed someone to give me permission to exhale, because I could not offer it to myself.

So, I started reading literature from the 12-step program, Emotions Anonymous, because I knew 12-step helped you break down something that had become unmanageable. In the Emotions Anonymous materials, I read a sentence that changed everything for me. It said:

We do not deserve to keep hurting ourselves.

Like a film sequence I saw myself in a closed loop that I couldn't exit: struggle, self-contempt, swirling . . . struggle, self-contempt, swirling . . .

Why can't I just get it together? Why can't I just make it all look like she does over there? Why am I struggling when this is what I've always wanted?

About a year ago, our church offices caught fire when a faulty copy machine shorted. The fire started around 4:00 a.m., so no one was injured, but the majority of the office space was a black crisp when the staff arrived to inspect the aftermath. One million dollars' worth of damage.

One of the pastors brought in a therapist to facilitate a conversation around the staff's experience of the fire, an opportunity to debrief. The therapist explained that some staff members might register the fire as an inconvenience, even a loss, while other staff members would internalize the fire as a trauma.

Trauma to one person isn't necessarily trauma to another, which is awfully confusing. How we internalize current life events is largely related to how we've internalized and flushed out past life events. If we've got big experiences stuck inside us, then current experiences will likely trigger those we're already carrying.

Like the critical line in breathing, feelings and experiences don't translate the same for everyone. What's hard about this is that we tend to look for validation from those around us, permission to feel what we're feeling. And so many of us have been told that what we're feeling just can't be right. *Because so many others have it so much worse, what I'm up against doesn't get to be difficult.*

Some of us lived in families where we were literally not allowed to have our own reactions to events. Some of us believe God would be disappointed if we struggled. Some of us will only ever feel what everyone else in the room is feeling because we would never trust that our own intuition or instinct could be valid.

We've let others talk us out of our experiences. We've let our ideas of God talk us out of our experiences. And we've talked ourselves out of our experiences.

When I read "We do not deserve to keep hurting ourselves," I knew my refusal to validate my current struggle was not only a way I had been hurting myself but also a "void in which I was drowning," to take a line from Psalm 18.

Drowning in a void. Doesn't that say it all? God knows we don't just drown in circumstances and crises. We drown in our own refusal to acknowledge and validate our struggle. We drown in toxic thinking. We drown in internal chaos. That void can be just as dangerous and deadly as any catastrophe.

Just as the psalmist did, I believed I had been offered a salvation, a hand reaching down to pull me out of the void and deliver me into a spacious place, a wide-open field, an expanse. From void to validation, surprised to be so loved.

That's the whole story.

Catastrophe or no catastrophe, if you are unhinged, disoriented, suffocating, or otherwise generally dragging, I'm inviting you to pull up a chair at this table.

It doesn't really matter to me what the outside of your life looks like. If the inside of you is struggling, this is your book, baby. I'm your girl.

Let's talk about how the Hard took up residence and how the stress piled up like stop-and-go traffic and how all of a sudden we woke up one morning and we realized we weren't doing well. Like, not well at all. The pain in our chest became the only thing we could see and feel.

Let's talk about how we might begin caring more how it feels on the inside than how it all looks on the outside.

Let's talk about how we might stop talking ourselves out of our own feelings, so that we can get some relief and freedom.

Let's talk about how we are both blessed and struggling. Struggle and gratitude are not two ends of a dichotomy. In God's world, they can simultaneously coexist.

Most of all, let's talk about how desperately so many of us need to let go of the ways in which we think we should be living so that we can actually, truly, really, live.

I'm not going to spend this book telling you how hard my life is because, the truth is, my life is gorgeous. Certifiably gorgeous.

I'm going to tell you how hard it is to feel like you're suffocating when your life *is* so gorgeous, and how badly I turned on myself in the midst of the Hard because I couldn't do better and be more. I punished myself for being human, for struggling, which is heartbreaking because it prolonged and intensified the struggle all the more.

My story, then, is a tribute to what happens when God reaches down to us with truth and we choose to reach back. And, also, what happens when we courageously extend a desperate hand in God's direction and he carries us into a broad grace. Void to validation.

Edna Pontellier is the heroine of my very favorite novel, *The Awakening*. Her life is privileged by most standards, but she struggles to find herself in the relentlessness of motherhood and marriage and the restrictive gender norms of the late nineteenth century. Barely able to tolerate her doting-yet-detached husband and two young children, Edna longs for a life she can't have. She longs to choose herself. So she strips down naked and walks out into the ocean, and she never comes back. She takes charge of her own life by ending it.

If we will not attend to the void in which we are drowning, we will disappear into it. That's the ugly truth. One way or another, unless we turn toward the struggle, it will suffocate us.

My friend Corrie and I were talking about *The Awakening* years ago, a favorite of hers too. She said something I've never forgotten, something I heard then, but I have actually begun to live now. She said, "We need to be people who come out of the water, like baptism. We go in—that's part of life—but not to stay. We go in and we emerge, cleansed and reborn."

How might we emerge from the Come Apart instead of letting it consume us? How might a truer, richer version of ourselves come up and out of that water? How might we hit our critical line and let go instead of holding our breath to the point of unconsciousness?

As long as we feel the need to hold our breath, hold it all together, we will never experience space, grace, breathing room. We'll be floundering in the void. But if we will let go, surrender, let the crash happen—validate that the struggle we are feeling actually exists—we just might be able to get the help we need to really live.

In our kitchen, we have a breakfast nook with an L-shaped bank of seating and an oval table. Normally, it's a hub of stickiness, which I actually love—the epicenter of a home with three crazy Tiny Tanks at the helm. Twice a week, though, Luke and Lane go to preschool, and I put Elle down for an early nap, and I sit at the nook with the house quiet. I light a candle in a mercury glass container and I drink coffee with plenty of cream. Usually I drink out of my pink mug that says "Amore" on it because it reminds me to believe God loves me with every sip. I open my laptop and get to work. Inevitably, when I'm engrossed in a thought, I will look down and see the rug under the table I'm working at. It's a vibrant tribal rug with dancing ladies in rows. Their arms are extended, holding scarves in each hand, a depiction of the scarf dance performed at weddings in the Middle East.

These women are my muse. Life as scarf dance.

To get there from here, I must wake up every morning and answer Christ's single most important question: Do you want to get well?

I believe in you,
Leeana

1

confessing
to the trees

The more we are able to embrace our sorrow and learn from it, the more we will also be capable of experiencing great joy. Yet to embrace our sorrow takes a great deal of courage. So often we try to soften or resist our pain.

—Emotions Anonymous

Perhaps it is better to wake up after all, even to suffer, rather than to remain a dupe to illusions all one's life.

—Kate Chopin, *The Awakening*

The cypress and pine—*Callitropsis macrocarpa* and *Pinus radiata*—of the Northern California coastline look like apparitions in the sea fog. Endemic to Monterey and neighboring Carmel, their ancient knuckles and gnarls reach through the mist. Creeping. Rising. Stretching.

God himself must be speechless when it comes to these trees. Earnest glory stripped naked right before your eyes.

Even in my woeful state, I can see how beautiful they are. They form a protective circle around me, warding off the world, and I feel safe enough in their confessional to say:

I wish everyone would just leave me alone.

As the words form in my head and leave my mouth, I know how bad they sound. Princess-y and melodramatic. Even I am annoyed at my desperation. Immediately, I want to find other words. Sunnier words. Something a little more socially acceptable to feel. Dinner party talk. After-church pleasantries.

One year earlier, when I was thirty-eight weeks and four days pregnant, I became a mother for the first time. My husband, Steve, and I welcomed boy/girl twins, Luke and Lane. I was immediately wild-eyed. They were the most gorgeous things I had ever seen, the most stunning gift a person could receive. Boy/girl twins. *So perfect*, everyone said.

In the year that followed, leading up to this moment on the beach, we all became wet ink. Our colors running into each other. I had no idea where I stopped and they started. Where they stopped and I started again. I felt as though we were artwork on a page that had been dunked in ice water— shockingly and abruptly cold—and our distinctions bled. Which is to say, I felt I had lost myself. How disillusioning to be struggling when things were *so perfect*.

I'm really good at making everything work, holding it all together, presenting well. I have always been able to muster. Always. I have always been able to override what's really going on inside me in order to keep things pleasant and lovely. Absolutely always.

In the Come Aparts of life, we find that we have lost some of our capacity to muster, some of our capacity to perform well. I guess this is another way of saying we've lost some of our capacity for BS. Ultimately, I think this is a good thing, especially for those of us who have become skilled in the art of BS over time. But it's also disorienting, when our ways of relating become threatened.

I began to feel so tired, so reduced on the inside, that the gap between what was happening inside and what I could present on the outside became harder and harder to manage. I tried to run, to keep that gap from closing, but it was always at my heels.

I would write really dark and dirgy things on my blog, and people who knew me would be surprised. *Wow, I had no idea that was going on for you. I had no idea you were feeling that way. I had no idea you were coming apart. You never seem like you're coming apart. You're so strong.*

I haven't always known how to inhabit my own feelings. I haven't always known how to let life be both hard and good. I haven't always known how to make peace with the paradoxes and texture of life. I'm still learning how to do that every day.

What's more is that I believed—as I had countless other times—that life was hard, not because it was simply hard, but because I was failing.

The struggle I felt indicated some sort of deficit in me and my abilities. After all, things were *so perfect*. I had a fledgling writing career. I had two babies. I had a condo in a cute beach town. Come on, people. Life had arrived!

The truth is, if you aren't at peace with what's "in here," then it does not matter one bit what's "out there." If your center is white-hot, then it doesn't matter what you drape over that center. The façade will be consumed.

Just days before my confession to the trees, I had been cleaning up after my now one-year-olds. Their latest sport was sending all kinds of food flying off their highchairs onto the floor. *Man overboard.* Nothing I did made any difference. Pats on the hand. Removing the food. *No, no, no,* Luke. *No, no, no,* Lane. It was all just hysterical to them.

For the one-gazillionth time, I sat down on the floor and began picking up bits of turkey, string cheese, banana, sucked-on peanut butter crackers. They watched me with great focus—four little eyes following my every move, as if I lived to entertain them—as I mindlessly piled their scraps into my palm.

What happens next will not surprise many of you. Because you have *so* been there. You've been on the floor, highly un-showered, picking up soggy crackers and mushed banana. You've realized, in some very primal part of your hypothalamus, that you too are hungry. In your attempt to keep the kids pleased in every way, you have forgotten your own need for food. That is, until you unconsciously start picking hair and carpet fuzz off the pieces of banana and shoving them in your mouth.

(This is what we call a low.)

I had assumed life would end up being slightly more razzle-dazzle. Turns out, it's me, resembling Charlize Theron in *Monster* in most every way, scavenging for discarded leftovers like some sort of feral forager. Oily, with bad roots. All from my new address: the floor.

When I think of myself in this state, I can summon no compassion. I can only summon contempt, which is the essence of the problem.

I want to be the girl in the Anthropologie catalog, the one who I believe to be the very best version of me. Perched on a tufted leather sofa, wearing impossibly skinny jeans with an effortlessly belted tunic. Loose curls. Accessorized with a bohemian ease. Eclectic yet not overdone. Likely gluten free. Showered, it goes without saying.

From my spot on the beach, I am longing to be "that girl." Not "this girl." And it hurts. I don't want anyone to see "this girl." This picking-hair-off-a-banana girl. This struggling heart. This mediocre mom. This everybody-leave-me-alone lack. The one who thought she could be so much more, and now ends up feeling like so much less. The one who is hiding, reduced.

I once heard educator and activist Parker Palmer say, "We are all heartbroken." He went so far as to say, the one thing he and the terrorists who drove planes into buildings on September 11, 2001, have in common is that "we are all heartbroken."

Well, except me, Parker Palmer. *I'm* not heartbroken. Good Christians aren't heartbroken. New mothers aren't heartbroken. Blessed blondes like me aren't heartbroken. You must be mistaken on that one. I'm just out here talking to the trees, wishing life would go away. Heartbroken, you say? Naaaaaah. Not me.

This is what I want to say. What I want to feel. What I wish were true. Some of us learned along the way that our pain is an inconvenience to others and probably to God too. We've also learned that faithful people don't come apart. Faithful people are stable.

We've also feared that if we turn toward that ache for even one moment, it will swallow us whole.

So we turn the other way—away from our own need—and we send the message to ourselves, for the countless time, that what's hurting us isn't valid. We've gagged the ache with Doritos and Diet Coke. We've covered it up with bronzer. We've smothered it with layers and layers of trying-too-hard. We've shut it up with the how-richly-blessed-we-are talk.

"I don't feel sorry for you," one woman told me when I had recently shared my angst with her. "You have two beautiful babies and a nice (enough) husband. I just don't feel sorry for you."

You don't need anyone to cosign on a Come Apart. In other words, you don't need to wait until someone else tells you that your particular struggle is worthy enough to call life hard. If it feels hard, then it's hard. If you're lost, it's OK to say it.

To not say it, I've found, is one of the most flagrant and egregious ways we hurt ourselves. Denying our truth.

There is so little in life we can actually control. Did you know that? We can't control our kids, our spouses, our friends, our parents, the government, the weather, God, the Bible, our pastors, our kids' friends, our friends' kids, our losses. We can't control people's perceptions of us. We can't even completely control our own bodies.

I know, I know. This is terrible news. I need a lot of control. Chaos makes me itch.

I remember sitting in the Middle East, texts coming in on my phone letting us know we had to limit all nonessential travel until further notice due to riotous infighting between the Shi'a and Sunni all over the island. I had a newborn. I had two three-year-olds pent up in the house because it was, approximately, two hundred and forty-six degrees outside. My phone rings and Steve lets me know he has to go on a trip.

These are the moments when you realize the one thing you can control is how you treat yourself. And that one thing can change everything.

Have we listened to ourselves as we would a dear friend, or are we treating ourselves as a hostile witness—distrusted, dishonest, discredited? Have we splintered off from and silenced the very source that could guide us home?

I do something radical. I assume Parker Palmer's right for just one second. I assume he's talking to me. I let "heartbroken" in.

I'm heartbroken that it's not feeling easier.

I'm heartbroken that I'm not better.

I'm heartbroken over these gorgeous, wide-eyed beings I've been given.

I'm heartbroken that I have no idea what I'm doing.

I'm heartbroken that I have no idea who I am.

I'm heartbroken that I can't breathe.

They say having an asthma attack feels like pushing and pulling air through a coffee straw stirrer. It's true. I've struggled with asthma since I was a toddler. When an attack comes, the effort required to breathe—to keep the air moving—is startling and consuming. Something that was once effortless and thoughtless has become labored and affected. Making you work to keep up.

When we're carrying unattended ache, we have to work to keep ahead of it. We live that coffee-straw-stirrer existence. Pushing and pulling the air so we don't suffocate from the small living. Then we stop. We go to the trees. We watch them move in the sea air. In one brave moment, we tell the truth. We confess. We take the first deep breath we've taken in memory.

I cry. An exhausted, grieved, wishing-it-were-different cry. I shake my head at my own inability to just pull myself together and get on with things. I feel how tired I really am. I walk in toward the low ache, which I had been fastidiously avoiding. I fall apart. I fall open.

This was the beginning of something for me, the reality that breathing room was available when—and only when—I faced the very thing I didn't want to face. In this case, my growing suspicion I wasn't doing well. I could no longer dismiss or override what I was feeling. This was a personal abandonment, a betrayal. We know it's not OK to bully other people, but somehow we forgot—or never learned—that it's not OK to bully ourselves.

How do we find the spacious place? The place where we accept ourselves—forgive ourselves, even? The place where we live with the profound sense we are loved? How do we find our way to *that* place? To *that* person?

We begin right where we are. With the ugly truth. With the ache. We confess we cannot get ourselves up off the floor. We admit our self-contempt. And we invite Christ to come and sit with us, perhaps offering a fuzz-free banana if we have one to spare.

We don't stay in the ache forever, of course. That would be despair. But we can't avoid the struggle, either. That would be denial. We have to turn toward the ache with even the tiniest desire to get well.

"There is a hole in your being," Henri Nouwen says, "like an abyss. You will never succeed in filling that hole because your needs are inexhaustible. You have to work around it so that gradually the abyss closes. Since the hole is so enormous and your anguish so deep, you will always be tempted to flee from it. There are two extremes to avoid: being completely absorbed in your pain and being distracted by so many things that you stay far away from the wound you want to heal."[1]

I begin to practice what it feels like to offer up my pain, because I could see the more I denied it, the more it controlled me. I begin to work around the abyss with a confession, a stripped down utterance of inconvenient truth. That's how things begin to change, I've learned. By standing toe-to-toe with the truth.

The sanctuary of trees bows and groans and exhales in the fog. Practicing their dance of approval. Like a scene from Lewis or Tolkien. Meanwhile, seven miles south, the Lone Cypress stretches out her gnarled arms over the ocean. Rebelliously reaching out for life.

2

talking back
to the brain vultures

I'm afraid that some times
you'll play lonely games too.
Games you can't win
'cause you'll play against you.

—Dr. Seuss

When everything—the car engine, the birds outside your
window, the sideways glance from your mother—is saying
Get. A. Life. you know you've got a problem.

It's like one of my friends experienced. In the hazy cave of
postpartum, the whirring rhythm of her breast pump sounded
just like "YOU'RE NOT BRAVE. YOU'RE NOT BRAVE.
YOU'RE NOT BRAVE."

In his book *Healing the Shame That Binds You*, John Bradshaw says the average, healthy human mind has 25,000 hours
of toxic tapes playing.

This is very discouraging, albeit not entirely surprising, news.

Toxic voices are those voices in our heads that want us to believe lies—sometimes subtle lies and sometimes downright boldface lies—keeping us paralyzed, isolated, anxious, insecure, churning, exhausted (because we are simultaneously believing these voices and constantly trying to prove them wrong), and often false.

The toxic voice is the dark voice of scarcity, while God's voice is the voice of abundance. The toxic voices tell us there will never be enough. There is only so much talent and achievement in the universe, so we must prove ourselves worthy of a portion, constantly. If someone has beauty or brains or a really nice butt, then it lessens our ability to have those things.

Those brain vultures are just waiting for a trigger moment. You know, a moment that confirms all our suspicions about ourselves. That we are never, and I mean *ever*, going to get our outfit right. That we are just not one of the people who "succeeds." That we are never going to be happy. That if we were one of the prettier people, we would be able to do life so much better. That our struggle is an indication of a deficiency. That we can't keep up. That we're destined for the bench while everyone else is enjoying the game.

All of this is so terribly unfair. It's the game you can't win, as Dr. Seuss says, because you play against you.[1] Talk about a void.

When we moved to Bahrain as a family, I put Luke and Lane in the child care on base every single morning. I was sick with pregnancy and exhaustion. It was 120 degrees outside. The pool at our temporary villa was so hot we couldn't go in it. It was Ramadan, which meant that most everything was closed until sunset. And I was truly, in a way I had not felt in my life before, desperate.

I drove the kids to the base every morning and I dropped them off and I would go back home and get back into bed and sleep. When I woke up, I'd cry, and then I'd go back to sleep.

The message, ringing so loudly in my ears that I couldn't hear *anything* else was, "HOW HORRIBLE TO NOT BE ABLE TO TAKE CARE OF YOUR OWN CHILDREN. WOW, THAT MUST BE SO DEPRESSING, BEING SUCH A FAILURE AND ALL." (All caps for emphasis.)

I was so conditioned to hearing these words—a lie that most likely originated when Luke and Lane were infants and I felt so entirely inadequate for the job—that I didn't even realize how much I was living out of them, how much I responded to situations and people and God and myself based on this lie instead of truth. I had no idea how deeply suffocated I felt by something so entirely false.

I've read the statistics on divorce after multiples. I've read all about the strain that two-at-a-time puts on a marriage, on a mother, on a family. And yet, I was *just sure* my own struggle was a direct result of my personal inadequacies.

That's the thing. When the brain vultures are circling, when they have their way, we aren't thinking straight or clearly. We are anxious and petrified and backed into a corner in the worst way. Life might be very difficult, but it's the toxic voices that are debilitating.

The brain vultures screeched in my ear, *promising* me they were right. They told me I mismanaged my children and my role as their mother. I believed them. I let them convince me I was roadkill.

I can see now that one lie jumped on the back of another lie, and before you know it, I had this totem of lies I was believing in, bowing down to even. I was letting it all own me, rule me. It takes a long time (not to mention therapy) to recover from believing something so entirely untrue.

A story took root in my mind and every bit of data I took in was skewed to confirm the story.

Didn't have the energy to make dinner tonight?
HOW SAD, YOU CAN'T TAKE CARE OF YOUR OWN CHILDREN.

Didn't have an activity planned for early reading readiness?
HOW SAD, YOU CAN'T TAKE CARE OF YOUR OWN CHILDREN.

Didn't stay up all night strangling the internet for toddler activities?
HOW SAD, YOU CAN'T TAKE CARE OF YOUR OWN CHILDREN.

Never mind that we had just gone through an exhausting move. Never mind that we were in a foreign country. Never mind that we were in a very different culture. Never mind that it was one million degrees outside so much of the time. Never mind that we didn't have a yard. Or Target. Never mind that I was pregnant. Never mind that my family and friends were 10,000 miles away. Never mind all that. I couldn't see it. I was irrational. Apparently, according to the brain vultures, it was just not OK to struggle. Any scent of difficulty, and they preyed. Do you see how impossible this is?

A few weeks ago my friend Jamie came to visit me. Bahrain is now behind us, but I still feel that voice right behind me.

Like, if I turn around too quickly, it's there to remind me I am just one moment away from letting Luke and Lane down in a catastrophic way.

I was telling Jamie how hard that time was for me, how I felt so wrong for taking them to the child care on base every morning and going back to bed. I said, "It was like I couldn't take care of them so I had to send them away so someone else could."

Without a blink Jamie added, "Instead of thinking you *were* taking care of them by giving them something fun to do every day while you recovered from the move."

It never occurred to me those events could actually form a totally different story line. Was it possible that, in fact, I had been caring for Luke and Lane by knowing I needed help and rest? Through Jamie's words, Christ offered me a way to remember those days differently, an opportunity to rewrite that story.

What's more, Jamie's words ripped me out of the swirling and churning and awakened me to the reality that perhaps I am perpetually being sold a bill of goods, unquestioned. And perhaps I might want to start questioning the validity of what's going on in my head. Perhaps my brain might need a reboot when it comes to some of these stories.

The brain vultures scream in absolutes. They speak in once-and-for-alls. They allow no space for complexity, paradox, or both/and. Toxic lies force us into either/or. The brain vultures say, "You are so weak." And what's worse, in our attempts to outrun our shame we will become desperate to prove, with every bit of trying-hard we can, "No I'm not. See, look, I'm strong. I'm strong. I'm strong." Because one little weakness immediately means deficiency.

What's far more true of all of us is that we are, actually, both weak and strong. We are God-image and we are human. We have within us the heavenly divine as well as the lowly dirt.

This is life. It doubles back on itself and gives you mourning and dancing in practically the very same moment. Beauty and struggle coexist. Loss and gain. Resilience and vulnerability.

Let go of the lies on the exhale, so we can take in the truth on the inhale.

I just assumed that because I was feeling inadequate as a mother, it was true. Final judgments were being cast in my head, and I was accepting them. You know what's true? I am a struggling mother *and* I am a soulful mother. And both are beautiful.

I had many ugly mothering moments in Bahrain. Luke and Lane covered in ice cream, sprawled out on the floor of the base food court, undone, fifty yards apart from each other. Me, 156 months pregnant, towing purse, backpacks, empty stroller, beverage—trying to figure out which way to run first. Everyone passing by offering comments like, "Wow, it looks like you've really got your hands full. And one more on the way. Wow."

Shut up.

These are the moments when I believe anyone else, everyone else, would be doing this so much better than I'm able. The shame is practically pooling around me. And then I do what I've learned to do in these moments, which is (1) secure the escapees, (2) breathe deeply, and then (3) reach out.

Because life is too hard for us to stand in the ring with ourselves.

I email someone who treats me with the kind of care I need to summon for myself in that moment, and I tell her how desperate it's all looking. And then, I get a note back that reminds me of the important truth about myself. And I'm able to access a place deeper than the shame—a true place—and I'm able to connect with the part of myself that knows, that truly believes, I am a soulful mother. In fact, I moved around the world so Luke and Lane wouldn't have to spend any more time than absolutely necessary away from their daddy.

Take that, brain vultures.

3

eating your shadow

I have a little shadow that goes in and out with me,
And what can be the use of him is more than I can see.

—Robert Louis Stevenson

Ten years ago, I married Steve, who is a Navy SEAL and who was, at the time of our wedding, home on leave from his tour in Bahrain. Eight days after our wedding, we flew back to Bahrain together and spent our first year of marriage in a kind of welcomed exile. When Steve wasn't working, we basked in each other's presence, like two cats in the sun.

While Steve saved the world, I luxuriated in large chunks of discretionary time—like I've never had previously or since—and the cavernousness was so incredibly quieting and revealing, I found a voice that had been inside me, but abandoned for too long. I found a soul voice, and I let her speak up and loudly, and all of this happened in such an unexpected way and in such an unexpected place.

How beautiful to go to a foreign place and therein find yourself.

Our first flat was located in a building called Capital Centre that looked out onto the Gulf from across King Faisal Highway and sat directly next door to the Meat Market where the locals shopped. I was always terrified of this market. A real blood-and-guts kind of place. I watched men carry huge skinless lambs with the feet chopped off. I smelled the horrific, third-world smells of fish in the desert sun. I saw the unwealthy Shi'a in their dusty, unbedazzled abayas going in and out for their week's meals.

I believed I didn't belong. I was afraid of what I'd see and smell in there. I was preferential to items in neat packages. So I crossed the street and went to Mega Mart instead.

This, my friends, is what we do. We will cross the street and pay ten times what we should just to stay in control. Until . . . there comes a day when all the things we will not face are at our heels causing such discomfort—such anxiety—that we finally acquiesce. Something has to give.

"I feel like I'm running, running, running all the time," I tell my friend Elaine. "I feel like something's chasing me and it's about to catch me." When this came out of my mouth, I knew I had finally put words to a deep urgency inside me that I had never been able to name before.

"What would happen if you just let whatever is chasing you overtake you? What if you just let the crash happen?" she says back to me.

This interchange hung onto me, like algae.

What am I running from?
What if I just stopped running?

The fear in all of us, I think, is that if we stop running, we will be crushed by what's at our heels. We perceive this huge force to be bearing down on us, coming to consume us.

We wake up at night, mind racing. We can't concentrate during the day, pulse elevated. We've hit our critical line, but we just can't let go. The unknown—even if the unknown is freedom—feels far too frightening and foreign.

"Maybe the thing you are most afraid of catching up to you isn't so bad after all. Maybe you'll find that what you're most afraid of isn't something to fear. Maybe if you just stop and let the crash happen, you'll see that what you were running from was, after all, just a shadow," Elaine says.

I couldn't stop thinking about this image. Me, trying to outrun something that was about to overtake me. Me, allowing whatever it is to catch up with me.

I shared this vision with Beth, my spiritual director, even telling her about the idea that perhaps it was just a shadow that was chasing me. She said, "Maybe you need to eat your shadow," introducing me to a concept popularized by Jung.

I did some reading to understand Jung's idea of the shadow a bit more, and I learned that our "shadow" is those parts of ourselves that we've rejected, those traits or characteristics that we've disassociated from, denied, even come to loathe.

The smell, the flesh, the raw, the blood. All of our humanity staring us right in the face. Our poverty of spirit.

We hate certain qualities in other people. We vow we will never be "that way." But somewhere, deep down, our contempt is actually a sign that we are, in fact, "that way" too.

We have rejected our inner fat girl, our inner star, our inner perfectionist, our inner slob, our inner vixen, our inner soccer mom. All because these feel like aspects of ourselves that we can't control, aspects of ourselves we're ashamed of, or aspects of ourselves that others have told us—subtly or overtly—aren't OK.

What if the best way to heal, to become whole, was not to try to reject or avoid these traits but to look at them, in the eyes, with compassion? What if we could turn toward all the parts of ourselves and say, like we say to each other in My Group, "I see you. I hear you. I love you."

"Inner liar: I see you. I hear you. I love you."
"Inner small-dog lover: I see you. I hear you. I love you."
"Inner hoarder: I see you. I hear you. I love you."
"Inner codependent: I see you. I hear you. I love you."
"Inner frantic fixer: I see you. I hear you. I love you."

The problem with rejecting certain parts of ourselves is that those parts show up again. They chase us, as a shadow would. The faster we run, the faster it follows. What we're doing, often unknowingly, is creating the perfect environment for fear, shame, contempt, and anxiety. Or worse.

As Brennan Manning wrote, "Judas could not face his shadow; Peter could. The latter befriended the impostor within; the former raged against him."[1]

What Jung suggests, what Elaine and Beth were both suggesting, was that I needed to stop, turn toward that shadow, and eat it. Let it all catch up to me—everything I was running from, and consume it all. Take in the parts of me I have adamantly turned against, believed I could never be, disapproved of, judged. Turn toward my inner Judas as well as my inner

Jesus. If I won't, if I don't, the shadow will keep chasing, and I will have to keep running.

Beth says to me, "Go into the kitchen and get out a big spoon and think about all the things you're trying to outrun in yourself, and just heap them into your mouth. See the re-integration as nourishment, fulfilling your soul hunger. See the acceptance and even compassion for your shadow as a way into wholeness."

I actually like the gruesomeness of it—chewing up and swallowing these bits of myself that I've bullied, silenced, pretended didn't belong to me.

As I sit down to name some of these parts of me that I have rejected, a complex truth arises. I see that I have—for so much of my life—been trying to outrun feeling "average," "common," "unremarkable." And yet, which I think is so true of too many of us, I have been very afraid of being "remarkable," "special," "exceptional" too.

I want to stand out, but not too much, of course. If I stand out too much, more will be expected of me. What if I can't meet those expectations? What if whatever I have to offer isn't enough? What if they realize I'm not who they thought I was? What if, in the end, I disappoint?

What I find, when I back up and look at all this, is a Catch-22, a very confined space from which to live. I don't want to be too small for fear of being forgotten and unimportant. I don't want to be too big for fear of being, ultimately, a letdown.

I begin to see that my personal version of scampering and running and dodging and pressing has most everything to do with my need to stay just ahead of this shadow that's chasing me. The shadow is everything I fear I could be: common and uncommon, remarkable and unremarkable, anonymous and known, brilliance and barnacle.

All the running offers is breathless anxiety.

What Christ is ultimately leading me toward is a turnabout to face what I most fear. What I'm trying to outrun, runs me. What I'm trying to disown, owns me. All the running does is make me false, which is why it's so exhausting. Trying to stay ahead of the truth wears us down. We become versions of ourselves instead of whole.

Like Adam and Eve, crouching in the Garden, we believe our only option is to run for cover. What if God is inviting me back to "naked and unashamed," a whole version of myself? No running. No hiding. No splitting off from myself.

"Stop wearing out your shoes," the prophet Jeremiah told his people.[2] Stop trying to outrun the truth.

I admit. I'm a shoe wearer-outer. I'd rather run in circles than stop and let the crash happen. I would rather run across the street than face my fears next door. But what if the thing I've been avoiding so adamantly next door is the very thing that would make me free?

Seven years after we had been stationed in Bahrain the first time, we received orders to go back. When I heard we would be returning, I determined I would go to the Meat Market. I decided I needed to face a fear, face the unknown or, at the very least, face something that had power over me.

With our new baby Elle in a frontpack, I walked the rows of flesh, trying not to slip on entrails. Luke and Lane were up ahead with Steve and my dad and stepmom who were visiting. Toothless fishermen flirted with us all. The smell was both nauseating and refreshing in its unapologetic-ness. No

Styrofoam packaging and Saran Wrap here. We were walking through raw life.

We bought shrimp by the kilos, veggies by the armful, and I made peace with a part of myself that was scared.

We made a huge shrimp boil with the shrimp we bought at the Meat Market. We filled our largest pot with water and Zatarain's and let the seasoning infuse the water for at least an hour or so. We dumped the shrimp into the boiling pot, and as soon as the water was rolling again, Steve fished the shrimp out as quickly as he could and got them on ice. My Louisiana-born dad presided over the pot and coached Steve—"Now! Pull them out now!"—with great joy. The grayish flesh turned plump and pink.

Shrimp boils have been a long-standing tradition in my family, and this particular shrimp boil was one of my all-time favorites. Watching my dad consume that Meat Market shrimp with the gustatory gusto he is known for. Hearing the call to prayer echoing into our villa from the neighborhood mosque two doors down while celebrating my Southern heritage around our table.

A beautiful convergence.

We made homemade remoulade sauce, cocktail sauce, chimichurri, and my family's own version of tartar sauce. We boiled corn in the flavored shrimp water. Kilos and kilos of shrimp down the hatch, gold that came from the place I had avoided.

The Meat Market feels like the nastiest, most foreign place on earth . . . until we go inside. We see that there's nourishment—like we've never encountered—waiting for us.

I'm working on this shadow-eating. I'm working on facing those parts of me that I've rejected, loathed, feared, neglected.

I'm working on heading into the Meat Market of my own soul and nosing around for the gold.

The pressure's off when we can ingest—with compassion and acceptance—our God-image and our dirt-self, our brilliance and our brokenness.

I am both exceptional and unexceptional, common and uncommon, remarkable and unremarkable. As Brennan Manning said about himself, "I am an angel with an incredible capacity for beer."³ And, the great thing is, it's OK. Why do we assume that our power lies only in the version of ourselves we deem most perfect?

I will disappoint people and I will inspire people. So will you. We don't have to run from our magic or our mundaneness. We turn toward it all, the beautiful mess, and we say, "Yes, I am all of that" and "I see you. I hear you. I love you."

This is one of life's greatest reliefs.

4

beginning again

Show me a day when the world wasn't new.
—Sister Barbara Hance

The other day I was driving Luke and Lane to preschool with Elle along for the ride. About eleven seconds after we pulled out of the driveway, Lane announced she wanted a doll to take with her to school. No doll in the car. I determined we were already on our way and she would have to play with the dolls in her classroom.

Commence Lane. Losing. Her. Mind. Bashing the seat in front of her with both heels. High-pitched screams that would make you think one of her arms spontaneously detached.

I ripped the steering wheel over and stopped the car on the steepest hill between our house and their school. I stomped on the emergency brake, threw my door open and flew out preparing to give Lane some godly wisdom about her choices. The incline of the street brought my door screaming shut and the corner caught me right in the back of the calf. Like a gunshot. Mom down.

Bent over in the middle of the street, trying to catch my breath, sweating, spewing unsavory sentiments, I felt practically rabid. I limped around and opened her door, breathless, and commenced a conversation with Lane between my pained panting. Trying to get words out while I groaned.

By this point, Lane was perfectly calm and looking at me like how I imagine she will look at me when she's fifteen. (*Geesh, Mom, you are so lame.*) Which, in fact, I was. Rendered lame by that (expletive of your choice) door.

All three of my kids looked at me as if *I* was the one who had lost my mind. Even Elle had popped her fingers out of her mouth and was staring at me aghast.

And then Luke says what everyone is already thinking: "Mommy, you're kind of scary."

I closed their door, limped back to my side of the car and waited by my door for a minute. Trying to breathe. Breathe. Breathe. Then I climbed back in the car, released the brake, and kept on driving. Because, after all, we still had to get to preschool.

When we pulled into the preschool parking lot, I was still breathless with anger and pain and wishing it were all prettier. I was still nursing the angst, protecting it like a precious. I felt deeply entitled to my self-pity.

One salvific sentence arrives. I know it is the way out, and yet I begrudge its arrival. Saint Benedict is whispering in my ear, "Always we begin again." Once more with emphasis and deep compassion, "Leeana, always we begin again."

Man, I hate letting go of my righteous indignation. I hate the audacity of grace, sometimes. I'm out for judgment, retribution, reckoning.

Saint Benedict invites me out of the corner I've backed myself into. He invites me into a much more spacious place. Breathe and begin again. In our parenting, in our marriages, with our bodies, in our recovery, in our thankfulness, in our prayers, in our attempts to cook a decent meal. Breathe and begin again.

I walk Luke and Lane into their class with Elle on my hip, and when we get inside, I put Elle down and whisper in Lane's ear, trying to let God ungrit my teeth: "I'm sorry I got crazy. I'm sorry we had a hard start this morning. I love you."

"OK, Mom," she says, her green eyes looking right into my green eyes. And she turns and walks into her class.

The tenderness is almost more than I can take. The ice in my veins turns liquid. Maybe that's why I'd like to nurture the tough. Bending down, looking into her eyes, feeling such deep compassion for her is so torturously tender.

I see, as I look at her, the scared child inside of me that is punching my feet into the back of the headrest, all triggered and tantrum-y. The hardest moment, as I put my face directly in front of Lane's precious face and feel my guilt, is then turning toward myself with the same compassion. *You lost your mind. You went to crazy town. You screamed. Your son thought you were scary. You wanted it all to be so much easier and it terrifies you when it's not. It's OK. You're OK. Let's try and begin again.*

Can I offer myself what God has already offered me: another chance? And another? And another? Can I let go of my own fear long enough to let some air into the room? Can I loosen the noose of self-contempt and receive the grace of starting over? Can I see that moving forward, however imperfectly, is so much braver than staying stuck?

I love Phoenix Jackson, the unlikely heroine of Eudora Welty's "A Worn Path." Over and over again elderly Phoenix Jackson must make the long journey to town to pick up the medicine her young grandson needs for a throat injury he sustained from swallowing lye.

The story is a journeying story—trudging, progressing, facing impediments and condescension, danger, poverty, a failing mind, dim eyes, an armed hunter, barbed wire.

Sometimes our desolations come in the form of oppression. More often, for many of us, our desolations come in the form of our sense that life has betrayed us in some way. In that betrayal, we are bereft, adrift, unable to tolerate that life can be both hard and good.

It doesn't so much matter that I blew it on the road to preschool. What matters is that I got up, looked into Lane's eyes, looked into my own soul, and decided to begin again. What matters is that I decided to keep trudging and, in the end, rise from the ashes.

We learn from Phoenix that even trudging can be an in-your-face miracle if we get up and do it. Trudging can get us down the worn path to the altar of prayer, receiving God's grace for today.

The secret is to get up every morning and, with intention, step into the broad grace we have been offered for this mercies-are-new day. And then do it again tomorrow. Like a ritual. Like a practice. Like recovery.

We never get over being human. We don't arrive. We don't reach mastery. We don't graduate in any way. We show up and participate day after day. Re-turning. Re-praying. Re-creating. Re-loving. Re-celebrating. Re-listening. Re-forgiving. Re-resting. Re-abstaining. Re-grieving. Re-breathing.

That's the only answer.

We get well by taking the small steps toward getting well. We learn to breathe by breathing. We learn to pray by praying. We learn to forgive by forgiving. We learn to accept by accepting. The miracle is in the one-foot-in-front-of-the-other participation.

If today, if this hour, if this year has not been what you had hoped, you can begin again. And, in fact, if today, if this hour, if this year was perfect, you still—must—begin again. We must wake up and choose to live in each minute, each day, each year. Moment by moment. Beginning again.

We must choose to love, to create, to breathe, to return, to quiet down, to believe. Over and over again.

And let's remind each other that none of us is too far gone in the same way that none of us has arrived. We're all in this beginning-again business together.

One of the most revolutionary things we can do is allow those around us to begin again. And, of course, allow ourselves. None of this is easy.

I'm in "baby step" land altogether too much, forgetting what I've already learned a thousand times. So I blow it. I mess up big time. I take a car door to the calf and turn positively septic. I feed the hungry grudge that's growing inside me. I nourish my rights to an easier day, an easier life.

And then, a gentle monk mouths these words to me: "Oh, Leeana. You are a child of God. Always we begin again."

I bow my head and say: *Here I am again, God, walking the worn path of need. Walking the worn path of your love. See you again tomorrow. Amen.*

5

borrowing prayers

So I kneeled down. But the words wouldn't come.
You can't pray a lie—I found that out.

—Huck Finn

In this internally intense season of life, I've had to completely relearn how to pray. When things became difficult and my capacity for BS so diminished, I just couldn't turn to God and pretend. So nothing came out.

I laid there on the ocean floor, looking up at the surface and the sunlight, and I was numb.

The poet Carrie Fountain writes about prayer: "I practiced rigorously. Just as I was getting good, I lost it."[1]

Unintentionally, I think we turn the sacred into something to get good at, a skill. Like tennis. Or chess. Or baking. And somehow, prayer gets lumped in with that must-master mentality. Then we see—we learn through our desperation—that prayer is much more about being human than being holy.

I could not find a single word for God that felt true. Perhaps this meant that somewhere inside I was angry that God had allowed the Hard. I felt betrayed a bit, by him, by life.

Has this ever happened to you? You just can't seem to find any kind of words that actually put sentiment to what you're experiencing. Everything that was ever said feels hollow, like a dumb joke on a greeting card. Like piety instead of a plea.

I had completely forgotten the insight of Thomas Merton and Saint Augustine: that the very desire to pray can be our most meaningful prayer. I had forgotten that prayer, like everything else in life, wasn't about my performance as much as my posture. I had forgotten that just turning my heart toward God in the desperation I felt was so much more important than any particular words I could manufacture.

And yet, I wanted words too, which isn't so wrong. It's OK to want to be able to put words to the chaos and give those words over as an offering. I wanted God to turn them over in his hands and send them back to me, collected, categorized, organized. Fixed.

None of this happened, of course. The words were not in me. Or maybe they were, but they were so buried, and I did not have the spiritual pickaxe needed to unearth and excavate.

I decided to hold out for true words instead of bullying myself into praying words I didn't believe or feel. Forcing ourselves to be false, especially to God, is a way we abandon ourselves. I needed to give myself permission to fall silent for a time until I could be truly honest.

In my silence, my spiritually congested silence there on the ocean floor, the words of e. e. cummings' poem "i thank You God for most this amazing" kept floating by, fish-like: "i who have died am alive again today."[2] These words must have come to me intuitively, dare I say even prophetically. They articulated what I wanted so deeply though I couldn't find my own words to say.

I wanted to be alive again today, to be awake and open to the world, to feel amazed and thankful, to feel the sun. I wanted to be able to *feel* the gratitude I knew was inside me somewhere. I wanted to come up and out of the water, alive and awakened.

When these words came to me, I prayed them. I would offer them, unedited, on faith that they were saying something for me I couldn't say for myself.

Of course, this is nothing new. The tradition of praying others' words, specifically the words of Scripture, has been around since the third century when the scholar Origen began to teach "Scripture as sacrament." His ideas later led to Saint Benedict's establishment of Lectio Divina as a monastic practice in the sixth century. Borrowing the words of Scripture and meditating on them was a way to experience Scripture as Living Word, finding truth for today in ancient words.

The found words were so meaningful to me that the "rules" of prayer became completely rewritten in my head and heart, and I began borrowing other prayers. Scripture, poems, song lyrics, bumper stickers. You name it:

He makes all things beautiful in its time . . . yet no one can fathom what God has done from beginning to end.[3]

Oh great God, be small enough to hear me now.[4]

O come, O come, Emmanuel.

God before us, God behind.

Sometimes I pray country music lines under my breath:

God bless the broken road . . .[5]

and

Jesus, take the wheel . . .[6]

It's fine. Pray in pictures that you cut out of a magazine. Pray in doodles. Pray in lines in the sand. I think the point here is that we start a conversation. We open up the dialogue in the way that we honestly can. Stuck silence feels small. Dialogue feels spacious.

Luke asks me, "Mom, is God in our mouth? Because that's the fastest way to get down into our hearts?" And I say YES. If we can find a way to get true words in our mouths, it's as if we are consuming Christ right into our being.

Sometimes I just say, "Goooooooooooooooooooooooddddddd dddddd" on the exhale. Partly because I was taught that saying it like this was blasphemous, but I've come to hear it and feel it as a way to ask for help. Don't hold back. Be raw with your language if needed. I don't think that's as big of a no-no as we were once led to believe.

Pray with your breath, the way the fourth-century church fathers began doing, with an economy of words that works with the inhale and the exhale. The most famous of these is:

Lord Jesus Christ, son of God, have mercy on me, a sinner.

You can use that one. Or you can use my paraphrase:

God, I'm completely nuts. Help me begin again.

Works perfectly on the inhale and exhale.

The absolute beauty of the breath prayer is that it takes our anxious mind and turns it to Jesus so our deeper selves can be revealed. The breath prayer is physiological in nature, which is so powerful. It helps our minds calm themselves like a chant or a mantra. Most every major religion has some kind of practice of meditation. The miracle of prayer is that it doesn't open us up to ourselves or to a void, it opens us up to Christ. Turning toward Christ is a miracle-waiting-to-happen.

Prayer is the language of the spacious place, and yet, the emotional and spiritual congestion can become so real and the fatigue behind our eyes so heavy that we just don't have any real words anymore. The path that once led us out into the open has been closed.

When we are most lost, the words of others can help us find our way back to ourselves. Borrowed prayers can be the words we didn't think we had, a prophetic voice that leads us toward what we are already feeling but couldn't articulate. Find a few lines, a phrase, a word or two that ring true for you in some way. It doesn't need to make sense to the outside observer. It doesn't have to be Scripture, either. The key is that it resonates. The poets find extraordinary ways to say the ordinary. Their words are so often the right ones that we can chew on, like God in our mouths.

Some of you have convinced yourselves it's too late for you. You've messed up too much. You've come back to the well for forgiveness too many times. You've tried and failed with this prayer thing so many times already. You've hurt people or you've been hurt too deeply. You've sent God away for good.

I am here to tell you that is the lie to keep you in the small-living space. The deficit. The squeeze. The inner bully says, *There isn't enough grace out there for you.*

One of the most spiritually significant things we can do, especially for those of us who have been in the church since our earliest memories, is to give ourselves the dignity of being honest and not faking our way to God.

The last thing God needs from any of us is our practiced pretending. So let yourself off the hook. Fall silent before forcing yourself to be false. Give some time and space to your soul. Borrow the words you need until the ones you want arrive.

6

sharing real life

When we honestly ask ourselves which person in our lives
means the most to us, we often find that it is those who,
instead of giving advice, solutions, or cures, have chosen
rather to share our pain and touch our wounds with a
warm and tender hand.

—Henri Nouwen

We had been living in Bahrain for four months, and it all felt
like a scald at that point. We had not yet received our household goods after the Navy's snafu of putting our belongings
in long-term storage back in San Diego (whoops!) instead
of on a boat to Bahrain. I was twenty-two weeks pregnant
and deeply fragile and we got the news that Steve's beloved
grandfather passed away.

Let me just stop right here and emphasize that so many
women handled their family's tour in Bahrain beautifully.
They had a sense of humor. They had an adventurous spirit.
They took belly-dancing lessons. They had nice skin.

I felt like I was just trying to get out of bed. Period.

When it came time to decide who would be traveling back to Arizona for the memorial service, it became clear it really didn't make sense for Luke and Lane and me to pack up and go—such long travel and such a short stay. Also, the family would be preparing Grandpa's house for sale during the few days they were all together, and two two-year-olds wouldn't have been helpful in that process.

I got it. But I didn't like it. And here's why: I felt myself getting angrier and angrier, and even a feeling of desperation started rattling around inside me. I tried to pay attention to what all that was about, though it was mostly—in the moment—about resenting Steve for having freedoms I didn't feel I had.

Ultimately, I realized how isolated I was feeling. And while we were settling in Bahrain and we were trying to make our house a home and that place our place, I was still vulnerable in all the worst ways. And not getting to be with family, while Steve was getting to, just made the scald burn.

I felt stuck there. If you've ever felt stuck, you know what a terrible feeling it is to believe you are trapped and powerless. I panicked a little and mostly took it all out on Steve, which he appreciated, I'm sure.

On top of it, I was there with the kids by myself for five days. And, of course, the morning Steve left, the battery in my car died, making me feel that much more vulnerable. You'd think getting a battery replaced in your car would be a simple matter. As it turns out, nothing is a simple matter in the Middle East.

I got through the events and emotions of those five days in the very ugly way you get through sometimes. Lacking hygiene and cussing under your breath. Eating fast food and sleeping with the lights on.

Still a bit tender and not totally on easy street, I heard this song:

> O come, O come, Emmanuel
> And ransom captive Israel
> That mourns in lonely exile here
> Until the Son of God appear
>
> O come, thou Dayspring, come and cheer
> Our spirits by thine advent here
> Disperse the gloomy clouds of night
> And death's dark shadows put to flight
>
> Rejoice! Rejoice!
> Emmanuel shall come to thee, O Israel
> Rejoice! Rejoice!
> Emmanuel shall come to thee, O Israel
>
> Rejoice!

It was October, but this song was on the CD playing in my car because I often listen to Christmas music year-round. The song was for someone who felt far away from home, someone who needed her spirits cheered, a person under gloomy clouds and dark shadows. Someone who was waiting for, longing for, a miracle. Someone who needed an injection of hope, no matter how humbly it arrived.

And I thought, especially after the tears started streaming down my cheeks, *Hey, maybe that's me.*

Emmanuel shall come to thee. The Dayspring is here. The Darkness Disperser. The Love. The Presence. The Company Keeper. He is here.

Rejoice!

What if the scald would lessen by degrees if I would just let Christ come sit with me in it? What if I stopped rehearsing the Hard and just borrowed the prayer, "O come, O come, Emmanuel"? What if I opened up my clenched hands allowing space for his touch?

The times when we have the least capacity to let others in are precisely the times when we need to open ourselves up the most. This is so hard. I'm the kind of person who, if I'm honest, would prefer control over help. But, I'm learning, I don't always get to be in control. And when the chaos enters, I better let myself spill open just a tad, so that the comfort can enter too. Exhale.

I realized God wanted to keep me company, even all the way in Bahrain, so when I began to feel more and more rigid, I would try to soften and ask God to come to me.

I didn't know how he would visit me. I just decided to allow a space where he could.

Three days later, I received a box in the mail from My Group back in San Diego. The customs form on this box should have read: "Detailed list of contents: love." Notes scrawled on napkins and Post-its, gifts for my children, perfectly pale pink nail polish, mix CDs, magazines, snacks from Target, sour candy.

I immediately realized Emmanuel, the Company Keeper, had come to me in a cardboard box.

Christ in the bread and wine of Sour Patch Kids, the sacrament of Archer Farms Tex Mex mix. Christ scrawled on napkins. Christ in love notes on Post-its.

Who says you shouldn't put God in a box.

This tender tribe reached all the way across oceans to hold onto me, which feels so radical in its generosity and acceptance.

Letting others in is a better way to live, even though it requires bringing down our defenses and allowing for the possibility that being seen and being known might be more meaningful than being in control.

For years I have been in a group with the girls who sent the box, and they have helped me learn that letting others in matters.

In some ways, it's simpler to keep people at arm's length. Much less complicated. But then there are those times when we are reduced and at our end and someone sends us a box that says, "I see you. I hear you. I love you," and the grace of being witnessed in our struggle is the very thing that gets us through.

I am jittery and nuts most of the time, and I worry—so deeply—that people will get to a part of me that somehow will no longer work for them. I worry that people will want too much from me, more than I can give. I worry that there will be a cost to letting others in, more than I can pay.

But you know what? It never works to isolate, to pretend, to shut down. It never works to try to be the one in control all the time. It never works to try to carry all of life's burdens alone.

I love the Scripture in Psalms that says "God makes homes for the homeless."[1] I believe God wants to bless me with a place where I feel known and loved. As I let these women in, I see a dwelling begin to form before my very eyes. I see how we are able to be a shelter to each other. I see how Christ helps me feel found through these women.

It all begins by letting them in.

Last month, my friend Tina invited me to stay with her in a condo they had been given for the night. The condo was

Downtown and I knew Tina would want to go out and stay up late and I just didn't know if I had it in me. When she asked, there were so many reasons why I couldn't go. It all felt like too much. So I told her no. But instead of it being a relief, I felt a gnawing. *Say yes to her. Say yes to her.*

Tina and I have such a long history together. We met when we were in the sixth grade, and I was wildly jealous of her small hands and long nails. I won't even talk about her skin and legs.

We have shared in so much of each other's lives, and that has meant we have had to hold on to our connection as twelve-year-olds, as sixteen-year-olds, as twenty-year-olds, and we have had to forge new ways of seeing each other and being with each other as life has changed. We've had to foster that old bond and we've had to forge a new bond too. We've had to learn how to see each other in today's light.

This hasn't always been the easiest work, and yet we have done it.

I talked to Steve about me going with Tina. *Sure*, he said. And I called Tina back and told her I was in. We wore our highest heels and carried our smallest purses. We put on a bold lip color and we walked out into the night together.

We shared lamb tacos and roasted beet salad and charcuterie. We talked for hours at a tiny corner table and bantered with our cute waiter. We went back to the condo and put on yoga pants and talked into the early hours of the next day. When we woke up, we walked to the Farmer's Market and, even though we had just a bit of time left together, ordered two cappuccinos each and shared a breakfast sandwich. I consciously let myself connect more deeply to her. I let myself be closer to her. And it felt really, really good.

I can go to My Group and share the deepest parts of my inner life, but sharing the day to day—letting connection happen over spontaneous evenings out—sometimes feels too chaotic, too out of my control.

Like so many other areas of my life, with these safe and tender women, I'm letting go a bit and letting the good thing come in. A bit more and a bit more. These women don't need perfect. They don't need pretend. They don't even need pretty or polished. They just need me to be open. Could I drop my guard, even just incrementally, and allow them closer, closer, closer? Not just into my internal world, but into my messy, real life.

So, I'm saying yes and thank you to all the women who take my baby out of my arms when they see me, who wipe down my kitchen counters, who help me at the park when I can't manage all my kids, who feed my kids because their snacks are always better, who coax me out for nights on the town, who let me see their messes, who see mine.

When I am feeling as exposed and vulnerable as I have ever felt, you are gentle. When I am manic and panicked and pinging off the walls, talking way too fast, and spinning stories about myself that don't hold up, you tell me I'm OK, I'm doing great, life is difficult and I'm pulling it off, and that—just perhaps—I might want to limit my caffeine intake ever so slightly.

I'm saying yes and thank you to the extraordinary True Beauties in my life who have loved me, who have inched their way in with great care.

You put me on the stretcher and cut a hole in the roof where Jesus is and lower me down. Herky jerky with sawdust in my hair, singing show tunes and complimenting me on my outfit, feeding me and praying for me. Laughing and crying with me. Thank you for getting me to Jesus. Thank you for taking me by the hand and helping me walk—one step at a time—into a better me.

Sometimes I'm scared to let you see me and love me. But when I do, I am always anchored and winged.

7

rejecting frantic

I have held many things in my hands, and I have lost them all; but whatever I have placed in God's hands, that I still possess.

—Martin Luther

Yesterday, I read something online that made me feel very defensive of my own work. The timing felt personal, like a sucker punch. Immediately, I texted my sister and Tina and Linsey and I told them to go read the offending piece. "Read this," I also told my mother-in-law who was here helping me with my kids while Steve was away, and I thrust my phone on her.

I was swirling, thinking through all the ways I could and should mount a bulletproof defense. I lurched into fix-it mode, frantic to exonerate myself, frantic to prove that in fact I was the one everyone should be listening to.

Tina called me and, knowing I was totally on the ledge, said, "This is not an urgent matter. No matter what it feels like, Leeana, this is not an urgent matter." She said a lot of other really smart things in that conversation too, but what I held in my head as a mantra was, "This is not an urgent matter."

Everything in me wanted to react.

How many times do we pick up something, assuming it's urgent, and take on the fixing of it when we never needed to grab it in the first place.

"Working hard and working out of a place of anxiety are not the same thing," Beth tells me. "If you can't breathe, stop. Never move or act out of that place. Wait until you can breathe."

In other words, ignore that impulse to make it all so urgent. Just flat out ignore it. Do the exact opposite of what that anxious defensiveness is convincing you that you must do. The. Exact. Opposite. Just be still.

Trying to defend myself, trying to fix this perceived problem, was doomed. All I was going to do by jumping into action was make it worse. I can see that now. In the moment, though, it felt like I would suffocate if I didn't solve, solve, solve.

When I'm around other people who are frantic and frenzied and anxious and think they have to solve everyone else's problems, it makes me highly annoyed. *Calm down, stop trying to fix everything, stop making everyone around you crazy*, I want to say. My annoyance with others' inability to relax, their out-of-control-ness, is such a clear indication of the rejection of those traits in myself.

The truth is, that frantic lunatic is me too.

I am forever juggling one too many objects at any given time in my day. Cell phone, car keys, base ID, purse, beverage (always, always a beverage), some toy-of-the-hour that each kid *must* have before leaving the house.

Something hanging from every finger. Jackets clinched under each arm. My ID between my teeth. My cell phone wedged between my chin and chest. My coffee mug squeezed between elbow and side. Two backpacks and a purse on one shoulder. All of this while trying to hold hands through the parking lot or push a stroller or both.

Without fail, something falls.

I drop the cell phone and the case explodes. The ID falls out of my teeth and into the gutter. The purse comes careening off my shoulder and lands with a thud on my crooked elbow, causing the coffee to splash out of the mug and onto my shoes. The car keys—every single time—try to escape. It's like the Tankersley Circus has come to town day after day after day.

Why doesn't she just carry less? I'd say about myself if I were watching me go by.

I want the courage to be un-frantic, to be un-frenzied, to be un-fidgety, to let go of all the desperation. I want to stop buying into the lie that it's all so urgent, that things will invariably fall apart if I'm not the one jumping in and holding them all together.

I'd like to let go of my need to be the one who knows. Urgently fixing is not acting out of wholeness; it's acting out of brokenness. *If I don't fix things, no one will. If I stop trying to manage everything, even for a second, the whole world will crash.*

But what happens when we try to keep control of everything? Something drops. Then something else. Our own health is damaged. A relationship we care about is damaged.

Our capacity to really enjoy our life is damaged. In the end, the people around us become resentful because they never asked us to be the savior of the universe. They just asked us to be present with them, breathing next to them, playing cards or having a snack with them.

I look to Christ who, last time I checked, has not asked me to do his job for him. What has Christ asked me to carry? If I'm honest, very little. In fact, if anything, over and over, he asks me to hand him anything I believe I possess.

He says, *Bring me your five loaves and two fish. Let me feed the crowds with your crumbs.*

The very act of letting go of our lunch is a powerful reminder of our humanity, our meanness, our tendency for defensiveness and anxious activating. We want to be the ones who know better, who feed the crowds, and we want the pleasure and satisfaction of everyone else seeing we know better too.

But this little plan—our Frantic Efforts to Appear Recovered[1]—will only backfire. Making us more frantic, and more, and more, and more.

If our cell phones are shattered, our shoes are covered in coffee, and our pinky finger is broken from carrying a twenty-pound purse, I wonder what our souls look like. I wonder what our relationships look like.

We listen by stopping. No more striving. We acknowledge we've hit our critical line, yet again. In the stillness we exhale, asking God to show us why we're running so hard, juggling so frantically, just sure we have to fix everything. We let go with a long, forceful exhale so we can get what our soul *really* needs on the inhale: space, love, broad grace, therapy.

Christ says, *Bring me the stale saltines. Bring me the sardine carcass. Bring me the meager, the humble, the modest. That little old lunch. And watch me be God. Watch me set a table of glory. You show up, and let me show off.*

What's cool is that God comes through. He makes weird little miracles happen—the kind of thing I could never dream up or manufacture. God multiplies when all I can see is division. So that's where I'm putting my money today. I'm believing that God will make a mighty meal where I could have only created a peasant's rations.

I woke up this morning and summoned a deep compassion for myself regarding yesterday's freak-out. I was scared. I felt like something very close to my heart was being threatened. And I reacted like I was cornered. The key is not that we become so evolved and transcendent that we never have a defensive moment again. The key is what we do when something triggers that defensiveness. Do we believe we must fix it all? Do we spring into action? Do we hatch a plan? Do we begin buzzing with self-protection? Or, can we ask God for the grace to STOP and go about our day as if what has just happened is not an urgent matter.

Today's urgent matters: nurturing my kids, focusing on my own work and not someone else's, revolutionary self-care, breathing (letting go on the exhale so I can be nourished on the inhale).

All other ground is sinking sand.

8

googling for help

God, grant me the serenity to accept the things I cannot change; courage to change the things I can; and the wisdom to know the difference.

—The Serenity Prayer

Most every writer I love is a recovering addict of some kind.

Here's my theory on recovering addicts, those who are actually staying sober: they've got a few secrets the rest of us don't.

First, they get, in a really profound way, that pretending is not something to be celebrated. I think this is actually revolutionary, and I also think most of us have no idea how to live this way.

Second, they understand we are recovering, always, and not recovered. Every day they have to nurture their sobriety. It's not something automatic. Even after years and years.

They have to get up with intention for today. They have to begin again.

Third, if you're a recovering addict, somehow—strangely—I believe you are learning how to have the right perspective of yourself. That you are both in need of grace and worthy of grace. That you are both a mess and a miracle. The rest of us are still trying to figure this out.

Fourth, recovering addicts have taken steps to pursue their own healing and yet know they are not responsible for healing themselves.

These people get the tenets of faith in a radical way. They understand grace. They get "no condemnation." They get the first shall be last and the last shall be first. They get caring for the least of these because they get that, at times, they have been the least of these. They get healing. They get that they are human and not God because they realized they couldn't fix themselves and they had to turn it all over to a Higher Power.

They have admitted to themselves that something in their life became unmanageable, which I believe is an extraordinarily courageous thing to do. Something we probably all need to do, if you ask me.

At this point in my life, when I'm over the easy-come-easy-go answers and the dangerous notion that if we just look at something long enough, we'll be able to simply fix it once and for all, I'm drawn to people who aren't trying to fix everyone else and, instead, are really serious about getting well themselves.

This non-fixing posture agrees with my spirit.

I've been thinking about the difference between fixing and healing.

Fixing is a solution, while healing is a process. Jesus healed in the New Testament. Sometimes in one shebang. But always with a person's process in mind. Not to wield control, but to whisper compassion. To show them the path of life instead of death, inviting them to participate in their own lives: "Do you want to get well?" he asks.

Fixing allows us to stay in control, which will never, ever work. We get to call the shots instead of having to truly and deeply relinquish. Fixing is our way of saying, *I want to feel better* instead of *I want to get better*.

Most of us know there's something inside us we need to face. We just need to get brave enough to let it rise up to the top. It's tied down in the deeper waters, waiting for us to cut it loose.

At a certain point—on the corner of "Lost" and "Overwhelmed"—I decided to go to the library by my house and begin reading the Big Book from AA. The only reason I can give as to why this seemed like a solution is that I knew AA taught you how to break down big, swirling issues into smaller steps. My mind was only able to come up with huge sweeping generalizations about myself—none of which were helpful or healthy—and I needed a new way of seeing, believing, thinking.

I was so deeply caught in that toxic loop of self vs. self that my energy was constantly going toward managing instead of being. The free-spirited soul inside me had been overshadowed by a constant measure of anxiousness.

Many of us need some way to break down the huge swirling mess inside us. We need an exit from the emotional maze, and yet we cannot will ourselves into wellness. We need to get some help.

In an act of taking care of myself—because I was fragile and tired—I decided I was powerless. I decided I could not save myself. I admire the help-seekers, and I decided I wanted to be a help-seeker. I wasn't going to be someone with all the answers. I was going to be someone who got help.

I went to AA's website and saw all the different Anonymous programs. As I scrolled down, one caught my eye: Emotions Anonymous. What was that? This was a group for people who felt their emotional lives had become unmanageable for any reason.

Um, yes.

I googled EA in San Diego and found a Craigslist ad for a new group starting literally blocks from my house. I emailed the leader letting her know I was interested and her email back seemed normal enough.

I drove to the building scared. Mostly scared this was the craziest idea I'd had yet and I was hopeless and this wasn't going to work. Mostly scared of myself and the desperation that kept rearing up in me.

The room smelled of a thousand cigarettes. The leader was Heather. She was right around my age, and she was kind. The only other person at the meeting besides Heather and me was a guy who was suffering from multiple addictions, homelessness, and felt that the root of his problems was his emotional life. This made a lot of sense. He had darty eyes and a twitch, and I was a little scared of him. Yet, I also saw he and I weren't entirely unlike each other.

I thought about what Parker Palmer had said (that we are all heartbroken), and I saw that Darty Eyes and I were really so much the same.

Heather began the meeting by reading about Step 1. She just read from a book about the nature of the step, about admitting we were powerless and things had become unmanageable and what it meant to start there, why we needed to start there before we could go anywhere else.

Heather then shared about her decades-long struggle with debilitating anxiety. Her agoraphobia and inability to drive, her struggle with always being the "identified patient," the one with the problems, while everyone in her life was there to take care of her and "help" her. In a word, she was broken, which just constantly reinforced how fixed everyone else was.

She shared about how this created an entire ecosystem in her family that was dysfunctional, how her mom lived to be her caretaker and how this ultimately led to her mother perpetuating the anxiety instead of empowering Heather to overcome it.

She talked about how some people have a real problem with Step 1 because it requires admitting right out of the gates that things are askew. Especially the part about admitting our powerlessness, which some people can just never get past. She said she had no problem with this whatsoever. In fact, it came as a relief to her, a confirmation even. To finally admit out loud that nothing she was doing, could do, or had done was fixing her. She couldn't, in her own power, change herself. She needed help. This just validated years of struggling to get better with no results.

When it was my turn to share, I cried. I talked about how sad I felt, how overwhelmed, how disappointed I was in myself for not doing better and being better, how lost I felt and how completely upended my world was. I told them I couldn't find my balance and I hated myself for it. I wanted to be more for my kids and I was convinced they deserved so much more—like a mother who wasn't a lunatic. I cried when I shared how deeply I loved them and how broken I felt as a woman and as a mother.

Heather just nodded.

The other guy twitched and darted his eyes every time I looked his way. I just kept reminding myself that he was heartbroken just like I was.

I came back a couple more times and cried every time, just saying the same thing over and over again when it was my turn to share.

After my third or fourth meeting, Heather and I were talking. She said we were losing our space at the meeting place and asked if I would want to continue meeting weekly at the coffee shop down the street.

I said yes and we hugged and I almost told her I loved her, except right as I was about to say it I realized how creepy I was being and how I didn't want to let go of her because she was this great kindness who had come to me via Google.

Through our meetings we found out we were both Navy wives. We decided to start working the steps together and just talking about how we were doing.

I started with Step 1 because that's where you start. Heather gave me a workbook with prompts to break down each step. So I worked through the questions for Step 1 and I came away realizing something profound: even the most blissful moments of my life have been tinged with some level of dis-ease.

At times, that angst has caused such grumbling discomfort that I have lashed out at people I love, I have chased after people who hurt me, I have isolated myself and insulated, I have rejected valuable parts of myself, and I have missed the moment.

Perhaps becoming a mother was what pushed me to say I'd had enough. I couldn't bear being lost in my own swirling world and missing even one second of my children. I just knew I couldn't risk it. The stakes were finally too high.

Is it possible I have a very special love inside me, a magic love that might explode and expand and catapult these three babies and me into something so full of Beauty that it would be God-on-earth? Maybe those toxic voices can't let that happen because it would mean love would win. And so they grind, and I get on their ride and it takes me nowhere but death. It takes me right out to the sea.

Through 12-Step I began to see that if I didn't believe God could help me, could actually come down and sit on the floor with me and help me, then there was really no point in believing at all. If my God wasn't actually a part of my real, true life, then I didn't have God.

Heather showed me what a relief it was to not have to figure it out. To let God figure it out. And to just invite him into the great mess of things and ask him to turn the endless sea of swirling water into some kind of wine.

I long to be free, to experience serenity, the peace that passes all understanding. I long for ease, deeply and daily.

One of life's great lessons is that we cannot fix ourselves. We need help. It feels needy to need help. Oh well. Let's get it anyway. Google is a great place to start. So is Step 1. "We admitted we were powerless—that our lives had become unmanageable."

(I believe in you.)

9

being nongodly

The Higher Power's plans are far superior to anything that my manipulating and scheming could bring about. What a relief not to be God!

—Emotions Anonymous

I began sweating and clawing at my throat when I recently watched an episode of *19 Kids and Counting* and saw Mrs. Duggar driving an 18-wheeler while she nursed a baby and conducted a live radio interview about her latest book. All while she was homeschooling the other eighteen Duggar kids who were rolling around the back of the vehicle.

And let me tell you, that woman was laughing and smiling and having a great time.

I literally felt my throat closing.

If I tried to do what Mrs. Duggar was doing in that scene, I would literally die from overstimulation. No joke. What one person can accomplish is the very same thing that will kill another. In cold blood.

At some point in my life, I got into this really crazy thinking that if I couldn't be more than human (hyper-productive, hyper-amazing, hyper-perfect Mrs. Duggar), then I was decidedly less than human. If I can't be superhuman, then I am subhuman.

This is what happened to Adam and Eve in the Garden. This is the age-old lie. The snake told them, "You can be like God." But when they ate the apple and tried to be like God (more than human), they realized their nakedness and felt great shame (less than human). Their only recourse was radical defendedness.

I've tried to outwit my own humanity, time and time again. All this trying and striving ever delivers is shame, the impulse to go into hiding behind our false competency.

The voice of shame is the voice of the serpent in the Garden: *You can be like God. You can know everything. You can be more than human. Just take the bait.* This sounds great. I can be more than human? I can be like God? I can do it all? Well, sign me up!

And we give in to the first and the greatest temptation of all time: to blur the distinction between humanity and God. We believe those voices telling us we can be, must be, in perfect control. We believe we should be all-knowing, all-able. And if we can't do it all, then we end up feeling like we can't do anything. Neither of which is true.[1]

I was driving recently and saw a fresh twenty-something walking down the street. She had on enviable boots and her hair was pulled back into a messy-on-purpose chignon and she carried a venti Starbucks and an I've-got-things-together sort of handbag. She wasn't drop-dead gorgeous or anything. She was just clean, freshly washed, clothed and in her right mind, and I was the farthest thing from such ease. I started crying right there at the red light, watching her float down the street while I felt like nothing more than raw meat.

Shame's siren song whispers in my ear, "You used to be able to handle it all. It's hard to believe you've become such a wreck."

Our house in San Diego sits in the midst of rolling hills, a more rural area of the city that used to be all citrus and avocado groves for miles. Our house was built in 1937 by the farmer who owned and tended the area.

I sit at the master bedroom window, behind my $30 turquoise desk, staring at our surroundings. I watch the wind lift the skirts of the trees. I watch the wind create a symphony of rustling palm fronds that builds and wanes like strings. I watch the wind carry blue jays and orioles. I watch the wind pull and push streaks of clouds.

I want to be the wind. Light. Carefree. Breathless in its wandering.

I want to be the wind. The force that controls and moves. I want to be the source. In charge of blowing things where I choose. Scattering when I want. Pushing doors open. Blowing down barriers.

I want to be the wind. I want to be the god. The brawn. The life. The power. The mover. The shaker. The beauty-maker.

I want to be the wind. The cause. The reason. The origin. The force. I want to compel. Make a path. Whip up. Swirl. Whirl. I want to move things my way.

I confess: I want to be the wind. But all my huffing and puffing just makes my soul asthmatic.

> The Spirit of life in Christ, like a strong wind, has magnificently cleared the air, freeing you from a fated lifetime of brutal tyranny at the hands of sin and death.[2]

God is the wind. I am the woman. God is the God. I am the human. When I practice being not God—nonGodly—I am trusting God's God-ness.

The truth is, I'm not always sure I can trust what he's doing up there. I'm not always sure I can trust that he will bring things to an acceptable resolution. I'm not always sure I can trust him with those I love. I'm not always sure I can trust him to fix the mess I'm staring at.

But I want to, and I believe that matters.

So I just keep asking God to help me take my grubby little hands off of my own life and everyone else's that I love, and let him be the strong God-wind. I ask God to help me forgive myself for being human. And I ask God to help me accept (which is the last stage of grief, incidentally) my role and his role as partners in this crazy world.

Most of the time, my humanity makes me feel so fleshy and exposed, which I don't particularly appreciate. As a human, I am not immune to grief, to struggle, to dark nights, to poor hygiene. I've had to accept all this. And yet, it's my humanity—my soft center—that makes me stop and take notice of moments like this:

Not too long after I saw the clean girl on the street, I was in the car again, creeping slowly down the stretch of road in Coronado that parallels the beach.

That day, I saw a miracle.

A big daddy was carrying his little girl. She was sandy and sun-smooched and her head bobbed up and down on his shoulder as he walked. Her limp arms were dangled over his shoulders as she slept.

"I get it," I said out loud in the car. "OK, I get it."

Some days we will feel pulverized. Absolutely meat-cleavered. Triggered in a thousand different ways. Our fretting about how we might do better or be more or how we could have avoided the struggle if we would have been a prettier or more talented person will only ever make things feel so much worse. We will zing and ping and ding around in a stratosphere that has nothing to do with what actually matters. We will exhaust ourselves to the point of paralysis.

The father-daughter moment broke into my zinging. Those two were about the deeper anchors of life: love, care, nurture, trust, grace.

The two of them were just walking down the street toward their car after a full day by the sea. Very simple and yet very profound. They are what is true. What remains. What matters. Holding and being held. Resting. Connecting. Loving and being loved. Beauty and the broad grace.

10

writing letters

Self-acceptance is my refusal to be in an adversarial relationship with myself.

—Nathanial Branden

Making amends is an idea popularized by the 9th step of the
12-step program. Making amends is about reaching out to
those who have been injured in some way by our behavior
and trying to restore what we have wrecked.

Amends is different from an apology.

An apology says, "I know I stole money from our family
savings account in order to gamble, and I'm sorry."

Amends says, "I know I stole money from our family savings account in order to gamble, and I've taken on a second
job to pay that money back."

Amends is not just words; it's engaging in restorative ac-
tions whenever possible. It's also a change in behavior.

In the 8th step, we are invited to make a list of all the persons we have harmed. What happens, so very often, is that our own name shows up somewhere on that list. Sometimes, right at the top.

We're beginning to see just how long we have been in the ring with ourselves. Our self-pity has kept us planted on the couch. Our worry has robbed us from experiencing pleasure. Our anger or rigidity at others mirrors the anger and rigidity we feel toward ourselves. Our need to please others has driven us to bully ourselves.

> Freedom means "we're not ruled or held captive by any one part of us."[1]

After Elle was born, I softened toward myself in a way that was significant. As if I were mothering her and mothering myself too. I was far away—in another world—holding my gorgeous new girl, chasing two crazy toddler darlings, and something broke loose. I saw that one of the few things I could control was how I treated myself. I saw I was gaining nothing, in fact losing everything, by refusing to be on my own team.

One of the common methods for making amends is writing the offended party a letter. I decided, as a gesture of grace and acceptance, to write a letter of amends to myself.

Before I wrote the letter, I thought about sitting with a very kind and funny and gentle eighty-year-old version of myself. I asked what she'd tell me. I tried to connect with that deeper, more soulful version of me, the one with henna on her hands and lines on her face and a big smile. She reaches toward me, taking my hand, and says, *I will show you the way*.

Dear Leeana,

I want to do things differently. This letter is my way of saying I'm sorry for being so hard on you, for simply assuming everyone else knew better.

I'm sorry I've held you responsible when things were Hard, and I've told you—over and over again and in a thousand different ways— you can't be trusted.

I'm sorry I stoked the fires of the old stories even though they were consuming you.

I'm sorry I didn't listen. I'm listening now.

Today is a new day. Today, I want more.

I want you to be brazen. Without shame.

I want you to live hotter-than-hot pink and cooler-than-cool aqua.

I want you to splash paint across today.

I want you to believe in mystery and wonder and wanderlust.

I want you to really see your own magic.

I want you to dance, for God's sake. Wild and free.

I want you to give without the fear of losing.

I want you to see yourself as a mother and wrap your arms around yourself and say, "You're doing it. You're doing great. I'm so proud of you."

I want you to hold those babies close and not spend one more second punishing yourself for what might have been better or different. Today is the love story. Today!

I want you to hold your husband and laugh at the days to come. These are the years.

I want you to become deeply porous so all the God-love can sink in. You don't need a perfectly smooth sur-face. Not anymore.

I want you to listen to that drumming within, those unique beats, and follow them.

I want you to stop running and breathe.

I want you to believe.

I will remind you love drives out fear. We can call out the voices of not-enough with their small-living lies, and we can rise above the shame.

I will whisper in your ear, "We do not deserve to keep hurting ourselves."

I will tell you over and over again you are beautiful even when it's impossible to believe, even when all you see is Monster staring back at you in the mirror.

I will champion you and remind you when you need to risk and remind you when you need to rest. Remember, sometimes resting is the biggest and bravest risk of all.

I will get you help when you need it, as a mother would for her child. I will help you laugh when you need to, as a friend would for a friend. I will create space for your true self, as God does for his creation.

I believe in you. Your ability to heal and become.

I believe in your ability to be small and quiet and to get up each morning and do the profound practices of caretaking and homemaking.

I believe in your ability to be big and inspiring and to get up each morning and say something that just might change someone's world, that just might bring them back to the Truth they've been missing.

I believe in your ability to hold on to what matters and let go of what doesn't.

I believe you will survive even if it's not all perfect.

I believe in your capacity and your limits.

I believe in your strengths and your weaknesses.
I believe in your joys and your sorrows.
I believe in your doubts and your assurances.
I believe you are a beautiful mother, even though you
fight that Truth.
I believe God delights in you.
Let yourself slip into great freedom.
I'm on your team. I'm honoring the Godness in you.
I'm honoring the dirt in you.

> *Keep breathing,*
> *Leeana*

11

stealing time like stephen king

The breeze at dawn
has secrets to tell you.
Don't go back to sleep.
You must ask
for what you really want.
Don't go back to sleep.

—Rumi

In my wallet I have a slip of paper from a fortune cookie I've carried around since 2007 when I was trying to make a big decision. It says, "Decide what you want and go for it."

I have to admit I believe God can speak through unexpected sources—paper in cookies, timely whispers from roadside signs, song lyrics, Twitter, and other burning bushes.

The "Decide what you want and go for it" message came to me at a time when I was trying to decide if I should quit my day job and pursue my writing career even though I had a whisper of an opportunity on my hands but not a full-fledged sure thing.

That one sentence said it all. I had to *decide what I wanted*. I had to name my desire.

Desire is a funky thing. We often skirt around it in lieu of what we "should" do, what we "need" to do, what we "must" do, even. We are skilled in the art of finding reasons why what we really want isn't actually what we really want and explaining away our heart's beat.

Mainly, I think, because heartbrokenness is hard. And when we name something we really want and then it doesn't happen—well, that's the best recipe I know for getting your heart broken.

So, we do this thing, this safe thing. We abdicate our desires. We relinquish, resign, step down from, hand over, give up, abandon.

I've done this before. I've decided to let someone else—someone who is much more productive or efficient or attractive or articulate or successful or whatever—handle it. I've avoided the fray for fear of heartbrokenness. But you know, I never save myself any trouble by abdicating my desires. I never find that approach more fulfilling.

I believe that dismissing what I really want (but believe I can't have or don't deserve) will make me feel better. What ends up happening is that I feel like I can't breathe. I feel like I've lost the beat. I feel like I let a small piece of myself die for safety's sake. I've turned away from the soul voice, the longing, and I've told it to hush up—that it's not helpful or wanted.

I'm not talking about indulging our every whim. No, not at all. In fact, that's the opposite of what I'm talking about. This is not about our appetites, which are frivolous and even, sometimes, careless. Our appetites are demanding and childish and usually leave us feeling worse for having them. At their best, our appetites are a manifestation of something deeper, some hunger we're longing to fill.

If we mix up appetites and desires—by overindulging our appetites *or* by depriving our desires—we will live hungry. In fact, sometimes the best thing we can do is get help understanding our appetites so that we can more fully experience our true desires.

Our desires come from that voice deep down inside that is unique to you, that longs to be heard, that is whispering important secrets to you about what really matters. True, gut-level desire, something God has written on your very soul. When we treat this voice like a liability, we are shutting something down in ourselves that's very hard to revive.

I'm always inspired by the part in *On Writing* when Stephen King talks about how he got *Carrie*, his first novel, written. He was living in a double-wide with his wife and his first child, working two—maybe even three—fairly unsavory jobs to make ends meet.

While the rest of his family slept, he would sneak away to this tiny utility room in the double-wide, and he would put a board on his lap and put a typewriter on the board, and he would write. He wrote the entire novel that way. While his family slept. Locked in a closet. With a board on his lap. And a typewriter on the board.

If you read Stephen King's whole story, you would see he had a hundred reasons why that particular time in his life was not the right time to write a novel. Anyone would have agreed. There were so many reasons why he should have waited. But Stephen King had decided what he wanted, and he was going for it. Even if he had to steal the time to do it.

Even without a swanky writing room and a beautiful new MacBook Pro? you ask. Yep. Even without the glitz.

If you are really brave, you're going to decide what you want and you're going to go for it. And, to be perfectly honest, it's probably not going to go that well. Not nearly as well as it did for Stephen King.

You probably won't write a bestseller on your first pass, though some of you will. You probably won't make the amount of money you thought you would if you simply followed your dreams. You probably won't gain the fame you had secretly thought you might. This is somewhat devastating because, here you've taken the trouble to decide what you want and you've gone for it. In some ways, it won't deliver. Not in the big, garish ways we had all hoped.

What the going for it will deliver, though, is something much more intangible, much more shrouded and mysterious. (Don't you hate that.)

Inside every one of us, there is a much wilder, freer, and more intuitive version of ourselves. She has her nose pierced or that tattoo we've always wanted. She is where possibilities reside. She is where, I'm convinced, some of our greatest truths are resting. She holds our most prophetic voice. She has a story to tell us if we'll listen. She has a story to tell the world if we'll clear some space for her to speak. She is our soul voice, our true self.

Deciding what you want and going for it will honor her and give her a voice. This is real living.

I can think of no other more significant way to find ourselves than to get to know that true self inside us. That rocker, artist, chef, mother earth, painter, singer, writer, philosopher, runner, poet, yoga teacher, hunter, high-powered executive, caregiver, quilter, humanitarian that's been quieted for too long.

We have, in the beautiful words of Sue Monk Kidd, "orphaned voices" in our souls, desires and experiences ignored. Hopes deferred. Stealing time pays homage to these voices. We intentionally turn our ear toward the deeper beats of our souls, a resonance that can be hard to hear below the noise, noise, noise.

I heard Maya Angelou (God rest her gorgeous soul) read her work at San Diego State University at least ten years ago. We were seated impossibly far away from the stage in that enormous gym, and the sound was unfortunate. What shot through all the din of straining and squinting was a six-foot-tall African American woman—then well into her seventies—who was dangerously and beguilingly aware of her own power.

Though we couldn't see it from where we were sitting, you were just sure she had a twinkle in her eye. In fact, you could hear that twinkle in her voice, in the way she danced through lines with her meter and with her hips.

She was captivating. Since that day, I have loved her and found such inspiration in her story, her writing, and her way of being—which is smooth and scandalous.

When her newest memoir released, I decided on a hard copy instead of reading it on my Kindle because I wanted to feel it, feel her, be able to see in print the way she grooves with words.

I was so engrossed in the book that I took my kids to McDonald's during the lunch rush so we would have to wait in the drive-thru line and I could read while we waited, children securely fastened in their seats.

Sometimes you've got to steal time for the things you love, the things that fill you up, your soul's deepest inspiration. The universe isn't going to hand you the time. You have to concoct a way to safely and legally and ethically (in other words, don't steal the time from your boss when you're getting paid to be working) steal a bit of time to fill up. McDonald's drive thru it is! I learned all this from Stephen King.

When we steal time to do the things we love, we find ourselves again and the parts of us that we want to protect and nourish. We find the parts of us that we don't want to let shame or fear or the brain vultures or any other kind of bullying silence.

Carve out a corner in this world, steal some time like Stephen King, and get to work. The world is waiting for you. Yes, small little everyday you. Yes, you. Worthy old you.

Put the board on your lap. Put the typewriter on the board. And get to work. Steal some time and show up to life. Do it because you want to tell a truer story.

12

getting life under your nails

I have woven a parachute out of everything broken.
—William Stafford

During the times in my life when I've felt exhausted, confused, backward, numb, or just generally depressed, I have found solace in creative space.

Very soon after Luke and Lane were born, I felt that growing tension inside, the ferocity and fear, the anxiousness. All that energy needed an outlet. All the disorientation needed an orientation. I am still very much that way, needing a channel for the inner frenzy. I feel best and most safe in the world when I have a creative place to put all that swirling into use.

I looked around and saw that other women were moving slowly, creaky and holding their breaths, other women were fading and disappearing into a cloud of "the shoulds," and I wondered if some dedicated time to reflect and express might do us all some good.

A famous writer was walking along the side of the road when he was struck by an oncoming van. Almost killed, he spent months and months in a hospital recuperating—miraculously. When asked what helped him in his recovery, he talked about his wife bringing his typewriter to the hospital room, and though he could barely sit up, he would type.

"It was the writing," he said, "that saved me."

I believe him. I believe God can bring salvation—healing, rescue—to our souls through our hands. So, on a hunch, I sent an email to a bunch of women inviting them to a found art workshop.

I told them I would collect found supplies (i.e., a lot of random junk) and we would get together and write and talk and then make something from all the scraps I had collected.

Found art helps me make sense of my faith—the idea that beauty can emerge in the most unexpected forms and from the most unexpected objects.

I believe in the redemption of found art, the truth that he is making "all things beautiful in its time . . . yet no one can fathom what God has done from beginning to end."[1] I'm (sort of) able to trust this more and more in my life. God is unfolding a work of beauty in us, but the beauty is made from castoffs, throwaways, reclaimed, even broken pieces. The beauty is not typically all that glamorous on first inspection. The beauty is rarely constructed from all the shiny stuff. And yet, it's there. Strangely, unexpectedly, magnificently there.

Life sometimes hands us Intense and Difficult, and we can run. But if we are serious about living the beauty, we will stay put and participate in the beauty scouting and the believing. We will try to trust that art is always in the making.

In the email, I told the women we would—assembled together—practice scouting the beauty, practice believing beauty is on its way. Insanely, women registered, which meant I actually had to collect supplies.

I decided I wanted to give every woman an empty frame to begin with, so I looked on Craigslist for a source. In retrospect, going alone to the Craigslist Killer's house was a bit of a manic decision I should have considered more fully before going. I called the man who had placed an ad on Craiglist for "A LOT OF EMPTY FRAMES." I called and asked him how many "A LOT" was. He said in a voice resembling pure gravel, "I don't know. A lot."

Good enough for me.

I said I'd drive to his house to look at what he had, and before we got off the phone he says, "You're not afraid of big dogs are you?"

Geesh.

While Luke and Lane napped and Steve watched football that fateful Sunday afternoon, I got in my car and drove to North County where this man's property was, and I knew, the closer I got, I had made a terrible mistake. I texted Steve the man's address so he'd be able to tell the search and rescue team where I had gone last.

The address led me to an electronic gate on a dirt road with a surveillance camera and a sign that read "KEEP OFF PROPERTY. VIOLATORS WILL BE SHOT." This message seemed congruent with the man I had talked to on the phone.

When I drove onto the property and the huge gate closed behind me, I got that dreaded feeling you get when you think someone is breaking into your house or following you. What's the feeling? Oh, yeah. Terror.

Huge, ninety-foot dogs chased my wheels, and when I saw the man who had placed the ad, the only word I could conjure was *Deliverance*.

I had no idea any of this existed in San Diego County.

The first gate was now way back down the dirt road and I assumed it was already squeaking shut, so my options at this point were limited. He directed me through another gate he closed behind me because he "didn't want the dogs to get out" and he brought me to the abandoned storeroom of frames.

I got out of my car and listened for the screams of the other clueless women who had answered the same ad from the Craigslist Killer and had been lured in—as I had—by the promise of a trunkload of empty picture frames.

I hurriedly said I'd take them all, and as I opened my SUV trunk, both of his huge dog-beasts jumped in, leapt into the backseat, and raced around from the front seat to the back-seat and back to the trunk again. My heart pounded and I strained to hear the cries for help.

Side by side we loaded every last frame into the car—in total about 150. I gave him some cash and got back in the car only to realize my cell had no reception.

The dogs jumped and scratched at my car door, and I felt like I might start screaming. The Craigslist Killer, as slowly as a person could perceptibly move, opened the gate. I raced down the dirt road, praying the second gate would also open.

When it did and my cell phone regained reception, I called Steve and yelled at him for being so careless with my life. How could he possibly let me go to this man's compound-of-doom by myself. And so on.

But I got the frames, which meant I had the beginnings of a workshop on my hands. The possibilities, even though I had threatened life and limb, were glorious.

There are seasons of life when we just need to keep breathing. That's the most subversive thing we can do. We might not feel like we're thriving because we aren't all jazz hands and high kicks. But sometimes hanging in there, staying in the game, is all that matters.

I wanted to create some space for all those who needed to breathe, who needed to feel their souls again. I had a hunch we could draft off each other's momentum.

I had some attendees and I had some frames. I spent afternoons with Luke and Lane scavenging for additional supplies, and when the time came for the workshop, I opened the doors to this old house a friend let me borrow for the night, and I began.

I read to the women and then gave them something to write about. Then I invited them to talk with each other about what discoveries or surprises had emerged in their writing.

We wrote and shared a couple more times and then we went back through our writing and highlighted what mattered, the words that bubbled up and named something that had previously been unnamed. Then we took a break, drank lots of coffee, ate whatever snacks I had offered, and laughed so loudly you could no longer hear the background music in the room.

I've found that when people are doing deep work, they need to take a break and cut loose. The laughter and coffee and snacks were what helped them spiral back in.

The words or phrases they mined from their writing would be the raw materials, the guidance, for their art project. I

arranged tables and tables of quirky objects—chair legs, bal-
usters, my Craigslist frames, finials, chipboard, as well as all
the necessary foundations too—glue guns, interesting papers,
ribbons, buttons, shells, and paints galore.

In the last ninety minutes of the workshop, the most al-
chemic thing would happen. Creative expression would arise
out of literally nothing. These amazing women, who had
just opened themselves up so beautifully, would capture their
realizations in paint and paper and wood and nails.

Invariably, one woman would be in the corner with the staple gun, just letting all kinds of sideways energy out through
the trigger. Another would be hammering and hammering
and hammering. It was just sort of an unspoken understanding that if you needed to pound something or break something
or smash something or shoot something, you had come to
the right place.

I would try to provide a Martha-Stewart-free zone, a space
that was much more about the process than the product. I
would remind them what we were doing was a prayer.

And then we'd all stand back and survey the prayers each
of us had just prayed through our hands and through our art,
and we would feel changed. We would all come through the
door worn and lost and we would leave looking as though
we had been rinsed off and resuscitated.

I started offering these workshops because I had a theory.
I believed that getting life under our nails helps us find our
way back to ourselves. Turns out, I was right. Also turns out,
tons of research has been done on this exact concept.

I read an article that said creating something with our
hands, whether it's throwing a piece of pottery, kneading
bread dough, planting flowers, or whittling, is "like taking

mental-health vitamins, building up resilience—our ability to bounce back from hardship—by reminding our brains that we can have some impact on the world around us."[2] The article goes on to claim exactly what I was wondering: "Modern science tells us one of the best cures for depression is good old-fashioned work with your hands."

This confirms so much of what I've experienced personally and in my own family. I have always loved the stories my mom has told me about her mother, Grandmother, who suffered from clinical depression in an era with little research about the disease.

I remember visiting Grandmother in Shreveport, Louisiana, in the home where my mother grew up. We'd sit in their living room and she would rest her shaking hands on the arms of an upholstered chair and she'd look off, through us all, through the house, out and beyond.

My mom would tell me about witnessing her mother's depression from the late 1940s through the mid 1980s, when Grandmother ultimately took her own life. About twice a year Grandmother would go away for a few weeks, where only Papa could visit her, and she'd return sedated. Gradually, she would reemerge. What always helped was putting her hands into life.

She would go to the orchid show and the African violet show, but she preferred to dig in the dirt and watch her own irises, camellias, daylilies, and spider lilies grow. She'd say, "I don't fool with roses; too much work to keep them happy. You get way more show, with way less work, with a camellia!"

When my mother moved from their family home in Louisiana to put down roots in California, she brought bulbs from Grandmother's garden. I grew up looking at Grandmother's daylilies and spider lilies, transported to San Diego all the way from Louisiana dirt.

When Grandmother's depression became more manifest and more debilitating, her best seasons involved creating. Her best therapy was painting. It kept the darkness away.

She found out about an invention called a paint roller, and she went to town painting every fixed surface green. Grandmother and Papa lived in their house forty-seven years, during which time every single room in the house except the kitchen and one yellow bathroom got some green. At that time, it was unthinkable to paint a mahogany chest or an oak table with green paint, but she did it. And the freedom was healing. Coming home from work, Papa never knew what he was going to find transformed.

One day he did come home to find that Grandmother had cut Mamie Eisenhower bangs on herself, my mom, and my mom's sister. She was always hands-on, whimsical, and not-so-predictable.

She is a testimony to me of how our hands can help our hearts, how our hands are compelled, intuitively, to heal us. When we feel dark inside, one way to turn on a light—even the smallest little bulb over there in the corner—is to put our hands into life. The inner darkness tries to convince us we're stone. This is the lie. We are flesh, and the creating reminds us of our flesh.

Over the two-and-a-half years between the time Luke and Lane were born and we left for Bahrain, I must have offered a dozen found art workshops.

Every single workshop stressed me out. Preparing and replenishing supplies. Picking up the coffee and keeping it hot. Setting up and tearing down. Finding any kind of CD that would work. Making sure the staple gun had the right kind of staples. Keeping an eye out for decorative papers on sale.

I would manically drink excessive amounts of caffeine all throughout the day, dragging my kids with me to do all the last-minute errands.

At some point, every single time, I would swear this was my last one.

I often felt strangled within hours of the workshop. Like this was the worst idea I'd ever had—besides visiting the Craigslist Killer alone—and why in the world did I think I could ever pull off this kind of venture with two babies. Cue the swirling.

Once in a while I'd have a great idea for a project and then I'd mess up the supplies or bring the wrong thing or explain it poorly and everyone would have to improvise and I would feel sick. For days. Just sick. And those voices would begin to howl and growl and I'd grow sicker and sicker, "introverting into my illness," as my friend Heather would say.

And the next morning I'd wake up to an email from a woman with a picture of her project already propped somewhere in her home—beside her bed or on her desk or hanging next to her bathroom mirror. I realized the experience, no matter how imperfect, mattered.

I knew some of these women's stories. Not all, but some. Some had crumbling marriages. Some had been through years of abuse. Some had lost babies. Some were so numb; they just smiled all the time with this waxy look. Some were lonely. And some, I didn't know. But when I had them write and then I had them share with the other women at their table, they cried.

I specifically remember the face of a beautiful woman I did not know. I watched her share some of her writing at her table and how the tears looked like lacquer on her gorgeous dark skin. How moved she was. How the other women around her leaned in, and how moved they all were too.

Even though I made some kind of in-my-own-mind egregious error in preparation for the night, the tears always reminded me that the spacious place was *already* prepared for us. Somehow the table had *already* been set. I just needed to open the door and bring some coffee.

I knew they had been brought to that room for the very same reason I had. Because they were drowning in some kind of sea, and they needed help catching their breath.

The temptation is to stay on the edges of life. But we can find a place of solace and belonging within ourselves by coming to the center, coming to the table, putting our hands in life. We can allow the creative process to wring the control and perfectionism right out of us. We can learn to be much more comfortable with a mess, learn to trust a process we can't fully control. A very spiritual practice.

For my college graduation gift, my mom had Grandmother's engagement ring restored and my birthstone added to the setting. I wear the ring on my right-hand ring finger, keeping her story with me.

She knew the inner darkness, and she found a way to the light. In the end, she could no longer fight. So now, I fight. I fight for me, but also for her too. I fight for the idea that we can live. Miraculously, soulfully live.

13

creating a room of one's own

The sweetest thing in all my life has been the longing . . .
to find the place where all the beauty came from.

—C. S. Lewis

I was reading the blog of a mixed media artist I follow and she was sharing pictures from her recent trip to Bali for a painting retreat. Painting poolside while snacking on luscious mango chutney and juice right out of the pineapple. Brushstrokes then backstroke. Brushstrokes then backstroke. For days.

When I saw the pictures, I was so completely intoxicated by the entire concept that I decided I must go on an art retreat. Immediately.

This is what I need. This is what I've been longing for. This is the answer. I kept saying, my blood pressure rising.

I am not really an activator by nature, so when I start activating—Bali or bust—it's usually a sign that I'm working out of a not-so-healthy place. I'm usually looking for a fix instead of taking the time to discern my deeper longing.

Because Bali was a bit beyond my reach, I found a retreat in the Portland area offered by an artist I admire and—with the most urgent compulsion welling up inside me—entered my credit card online and signed up. Within minutes, I had roped a friend into going with me.

Then, I stopped and actually read the description of the retreat. The weekend was more about inspiration and, upon closer examination, was not about actual creating at all.

So I asked for my money back, and then I decided, since I couldn't go to Bali and Portland wasn't producing for me, I would rip down the tool shed attached to the back of our garage and build myself an art studio instead. Never mind that I can't even get in the shower by myself, if I could just build a beautiful studio, and if I could go there every day and create in solitude, then I would feel cured.

In a matter of fifty-six minutes, I had researched art retreats in Bali, actually registered for a retreat in Portland, found a friend to go with me, canceled my trip to Portland, and made a plan to remodel a shed into a garage art studio.

Steve was so exhausted.

When I finally came down off this manic trip, I still didn't have a painting retreat planned or a studio in the works. I did have an edgy self-contempt, embarrassed by my anxious outburst.

When I stop, and breathe, and turn toward myself, what I usually discover is an essential part of me in need.

None of this is wrong. In fact, it all makes sense. Christ has already elbowed out the spacious place, the broad grace, on our behalf. But so often we can't find our way to it. Something stands in our way. Sometimes *we* stand in our way. But our soul is trying to point us home.

We try to fix because we feel broken. I'm sure I felt suffocated by life, and I just wanted that elusive breathing room. In that moment, it felt like, if I could just get to Bali, I could breathe. If I could just get to Portland, I could breathe. If I could just tear down the tool shed and build my own room, I could breathe. If I could do any one of those things, I would know exactly who I am and where I belong.

What I didn't realize is that if I would just put my computer away, put my credit card away, put all my planning away, and listen, I might hear the truth.

In the Hebrew Scriptures, one of the names for God is *Ha-Makom* meaning "the omnipresent," literally translated "The Place." This name for God is often used in the traditional Jewish sentiment offered to someone in grief, "*HaMakom yenachem et'chem*" meaning "May The Place comfort you." May your struggle be met with ultimate belonging.

Leeana, you do not have to drown in the void. I am The Place. I offer you belonging here and now. I, The Place, am what you long for.

In her essay "A Room of One's Own," Virginia Woolf admonishes us to find a space in this big crazy world, claim it, and return to it. This will help us find ourselves. This will help give us a voice, or give us back our voice if we have lost it.

Woolf intended this piece to call forth women writers who were quieted in a patriarchal industry. Her message was: let's find our place—both literally and figuratively—and in doing so, discover our voices. Her point was: "To be placeless is to be silenced."[1] When we are without a sense of place, we are missing out on a powerful part of our identity.

Some of us would benefit from a physical space in our homes that could be all ours, a place that reminds us we live there too, our needs are important too, and we haven't been run out and run over by every other living thing under our roof. Some of us need to adamantly announce that the dog food, the tools, and the electronics are no longer going to take priority over our souls.

In a particularly squeezy time in these last four years, a friend offered me a room in an old house she was using as a place of outreach to homeless women. Ironically, during that season, Steve, Luke, Lane, and I were living with my mom, so perhaps my friend saw that I was part of her target audience.

I would go there, when I could afford a babysitter, and I would sit on the floor and paint or cut up magazines, or write, or sleep. Just knowing I had a place brought comfort.

I saw the power of a space to make a person feel protected, nourished, creative, and free. I saw how the space could help you dream again, get your hands moving again. I saw how a space could become an altar, a place to commemorate, pray, experience the holy, a place to return to, like a pilgrimage.

We long to know who we are, to know what we love, to be settled, to be home. Our places help us hash all that out, I believe. Where we like to go. What we want to be surrounded by when we get there. Who we want to become when we grow up. Our places can be where we practice the ritual of taking our soul pulse, trying out our voice, and attending to our needs.

But—and this is what I'm learning every single day—I don't think any literal place can deliver a sense of home or belonging if we have not first found that within.

What if we could access the place inside ourselves that is warm, nurturing, welcoming, and comforting? What if we could experience a space that is a refuge for ourselves in this weary world? And what if we could go to that place, often, and receive love, compassion, and tenderness no matter what in the world is going on? No matter how acutely life is coming apart.

What if that space already exists? What if we allowed Christ to lead us there?

More than an art studio on the back of my garage (though that would be completely and insanely amazing, I won't lie), Bali, and Portland combined, I long for a place inside myself that is home. I long for The Place.

I can't wait to go on a painting retreat—to Bali, to Portland, or wherever. I can't wait until the day when we can rip down that ugly, old, brown tool shed that's halfway falling down anyway and, in its place, construct a beautiful art studio with aqua walls and a painted cement floor and open shelves full of possibilities just waiting for me.

I can't wait to invite you to come over and create with me in my studio where light will be flooding in and rolls of kraft paper and chipboard will never end. We'll drink hot coffee from our Amore mugs and we'll laugh and cry and say things like, "We are the luckiest."

I can't wait.

For now, I will nurture the room of one's own within, the one I am still learning to recognize, the wellspring of worth. It's been there all along, I see, and I've longed for it and longed for it some more. *HaMakom* is showing me the way back home, The Place where I belong.

14

piercing the
membrane

Life shrinks or expands in proportion to one's courage.

—Anais Nin

I decided to go see a spiritual director.

Since we returned from Bahrain, I've been feeling so exhausted—so old-feeling and trudgy—that I'm practically sure something is wrong with me.

In the morning, I step out of bed and it feels like all the bones in my feet are made of eggshells. And then I look in the mirror and my eyes are literally melting down my face. I greet my children and have to think to remember their names.

"Perhaps, and this is just a suggestion of course, you might want to call your doctor," my mom mentions.

So I call my doctor's office, and when the receptionist asks the nature of my appointment, I tell her I'm borderline catatonic. "OK great," she says, "I'll go ahead and put that down in your chart," trying to maintain cheeriness.

After blood work and a thyroid check and a thorough interrogation, my doctor determines I am suffering from "feeling tired." While this is certainly accurate, I was hoping I could get a more specific diagnosis instead of having to do what I did next—I decided to get the help of another kind of expert. Someone trained in the art of looking at the whole. I called Beth, a spiritual director I met with once, years ago, and I asked if we could meet.

A spiritual director is someone who helps you see, hear, taste, smell, touch God in your life. They are both companion and guide, helping you scout God's Godness and your true self. This is an especially valuable relationship when you are in a time of discernment, recovery, or transition. So, basically, all the time.

I find it somewhat needy to always need help, the way I do. I kind of roll my eyes at myself sometimes, like, *Here we go again. What's next? Will we be researching witch doctors on Yelp by the end of the month?* But I do it, because I've learned along the way that staying in the closed loop of my own mind is a doomed strategy.

I go to Beth's house and follow her directions to walk to the back of the house where her patio sits in the middle of a eucalyptus-lined canyon. A gang of ceramic monkeys riding surfboards smile at me as I walk down the stairs toward her back door. I knock and Beth appears, her dreads pulled halfway up, as serene as a human cloud. She hugged me in a way that made me want to cry because I felt like I had arrived at a very unconventional sort of womb.

We sat at her outdoor table and I kept my oversized sunglasses on while the wind came up from the canyon floor, pushing up, and the heat from the sun pushed down, creating the pocket where she and I sat facing each other. She said we'd bow our heads in a moment of silence and then she'd break the silence with a prayer. Just these words, just the pocket we were in, was enough to usher the tears.

I told her the whole story about becoming a mother and about moving to Bahrain and not knowing how to take care of my kids there and then moving back to San Diego and trying to start over here and about how ferocious it all felt. I told her I was exhausted and scared, and no matter what I knew to be true about myself and about God, the truth couldn't crack into the craziness. Everything felt enormous, and I felt like a Lilliputian in proportion to my own life.

"Maybe this is a time to think about mothering yourself. Elbowing out some space on your own behalf. Nurturing yourself into recovery. Nourishing the depleted parts of you," Beth says.

"Leeana, you are bleeding out." She looks right into my soul. "The life will continue to drain out of you if you don't stop and let yourself recover. You've got to clear out that space for yourself."

This feeling—the feeling of losing my breath, my spirit, my vitality, my zest—is what terrifies me. The bleeding out. I run to try to stay ahead of it, to prove that I'm not fading away, but the more I run, the more my entire system is failing.

I remember the woman in the New Testament Scriptures who, exiled from years of bleeding, reaches to touch Christ in a sea of people. If she can just touch the edge of his clothes, she believes she will be healed.

As her hand catches his garment, she is immediately healed from her issue and she feels in her spirit as though she is freed from suffering.

Blood is so gory, so human, ready to drain from us at any second. Blood is vulnerability in liquid form. I love that the Bible includes a story about blood, about a woman who is bleeding. How personal. I also love the picture of her reaching out to Christ, desperate, lost in the crowd.

When he feels she has touched him, he turns and wants to know who it was. His disciples basically tell Jesus he's dumb for asking. *An entire crowd is pushing in on you. Everyone is touching you.* But he stops to recognize the one. He turns everyone's eyes on this woman who has been marginalized and he calls her daughter.[1] Daughter, go in peace.

Jesus is so good like that. Saving the one. Even if, especially if, that one has been discarded by everyone else.

He could have healed her physically without bringing any attention to her whatsoever. He could have just let her slip away. Instead, he tells every single person in attendance that day, "See her? The one you have cast aside? She belongs."

Beth-with-Dreads was right. I was bleeding out, and the only thing I knew to do was reach out and touch someone who could possibly help. When we reach out, we pierce the membrane that has formed around us and we create just enough space for someone else to reach in.

This is our lifeline.

I was at My Group last night and one friend said, "I've been praying for lifelines." She is the mother of three very young children, all born right in a row, one of whom doesn't really feel the need to sleep. She's needed some space, some breathing room, and she's prayed that God would show her how she might be saved. I find this to be such a courageous and inspirational prayer. "I'm underwater," she tells us, "and I need someone to throw me a lifeline."

116

God threw her a lifeline in the form of a local MOPS group at a church less than a mile from her house. The funny thing is, she didn't really see herself as someone who "needed" MOPS. Until she went. And she realized that she was sitting at a table with eight other women who had prayed that same prayer, and God brought them all together.

Lifelines don't always arrive in the packages we had expected or planned. Often, the lifelines meet in a cafeteria with fluorescent lighting. They are almost always an invitation for us to accept our own neediness.

I am in need, just like this woman next to me who will not stop talking to me. I am in need, just like her over there with the bad shoes. I am in need, just like that one with her shirt on wrong side out. Here we are. All of us. In need. Pass the coffee, please.

To the extent that I am unwilling to admit my own neediness, to that same extent I will not be able to experience the mutuality and interdependence of community. Community is not having people around you. Community is not even having people into your home. Community is the mutuality of needs expressed and needs met. Reaching out and allowing someone to reach back.

Some of us are waiting until we have the energy, the resources, the space, the right words, or the time to reach out. This is a ruse. It's like saying you're going to get in shape a bit more before you hire that personal trainer you need. This is the kind of thinking that allows us to keep ourselves at a safe distance from support. This is what we call self-sabotage.

The etymology of "reach out" takes us back to roots meaning "to extend oneself" and "torture," as in the idea of putting one's body on the rack. Well, doesn't that say it all.

Reaching out—the whole point of it—is that we do it in our most blind, most lost, most wordless, most depleted moments. Even though it doesn't feel good. Even though it feels like we're really extending ourselves beyond what's comfortable, dislocating those safely intact joints. Even though it feels torturous to be in need *yet again*.

We practice asking for help over and over so that next time, we don't wait so long to get it. We allow God to bring us the help in ways that we would not have planned or contrived.

We find ourselves in a room full of women we don't know, and after about fifteen minutes we realize God had been saving us a seat. We find ourselves sitting on a relative stranger's patio, sobbing audibly, while ceramic monkeys look on, and we realize we are holding the hand of Jesus Christ in a woman's body with dreads.

Reaching out can look like a lot of different things. Reaching out to a trusted friend, someone who will listen instead of advise. Someone who will simply stay in the room and breathe instead of trying to fix it all for us.

Reaching out might mean picking up the thousand-pound phone and calling a professional. Someone who is trained in spiritual direction or therapy or trauma recovery or making people laugh.

Reaching out might mean calling your sponsor or Your Group.

Reaching out could be attending that class or workshop you've been avoiding, choosing to gain tools instead of ignoring the issue.

Reaching out might be turning toward Christ with a borrowed prayer.

Reaching out is sending the following text: "Help. I'm

scared. Pray for me today. I don't believe anymore. I need you to believe for me."

Reaching out is one moment that gives us something to build on, the moment that interrupts our toxic trajectory and creates a momentum of health.

Reaching out is a step toward rescue.

These days, when I realize *it's one of those days* when things are growing grimmer and grimier at my house and I want to take out my self-contempt on anything and everything in my path, I try to remind myself that this is part of living. The down days. I haven't failed because I'm struggling. I'm just struggling. So what do I need to do?

I need to turn to myself as a mother would her child.

I think about Lane coming into our room in the middle of the night, desperately trying to breathe after croup descended on her in her sleep without warning. I scoop her up and race to the Emergency Room, holding her hand while I drive, asking her to squeeze my hand when she sees a green light, squeeze my hand when she sees a red light. I run her inside, fevery and wheezing, and I get her care.

I don't scold her for being ill. I don't roll my eyes at the inconvenience. I don't say, "Can't you get it together, Lane? This is so like you. To need all this help." I help her. Because I'm her mother. Because she needs me. Because she is my very heart in a four-year-old body. Because she can't breathe.

Beth was asking me to think of myself in those same terms. Not as an inconvenience, but both as a child who is in need, and also as the strong mother who holds her child close and protects her with unending compassion.

If I can't breathe, I need to get myself to the care that I need. As I would for my darling Lane. Period.

I can talk myself into "sucking it up" and "not making such a big deal out of everything." Sure. But if I would have stuffed down all my need, I would have robbed myself of Beth-with-Dreads reaching back to me and guiding me toward fierce gentleness. I would have missed her plea, the Divine plea—*Come to me, all you who are weary and burdened*—to allow myself the dignity of rest and recovery.

I could have stayed stuck in the cycle of bleeding. Instead, I received the gift of *Daughter, go in peace.*

15

wielding power tools

The best way out is always through.
—Robert Frost

We were waiting to hear if Steve would be getting orders to the Middle East and, also, if Luke, Lane, and I would be able to join him.

The government put a Stop Movement Order on all families going to Bahrain since the Arab Spring had trickled its way into Bahrain and the Shi'a were rising up for civil rights. "The Troubles," as it was referred to, spiked on February 14, 2011, on "The Day of Rage," when Shi'a protests turned violent throughout the island.

While we were waiting, I found out I was pregnant.

The early weeks were going smoothly, but the morning of our first doctor's appointment, I woke up and was bleeding. We went in for the scheduled ultrasound, and the nurse shook her head and said, "I'm 99 percent certain this is not a viable pregnancy. See here," she said pointing to the picture on the screen, "this is just a yolk sack, but the baby hasn't formed properly. I don't see a heartbeat."

I was nine weeks pregnant, and somehow I had wrongly convinced myself that if you get past six or seven weeks, you're home free.

I was numb. Silent. Like something inside me had been muted. I was confused. Had we lost a baby or a yolk sack?

I thought of the Dickinson poem: "After great pain, a formal feeling comes . . . / First chill, then stupor, then the letting go."[1]

When I was quiet those lines would run through my head. And these from John Greenleaf Whittier: "For of all sad words of tongue or pen, / The saddest are these: 'It might have been.'"[2]

Grieving is the process of recognizing the loss of what might have been. Never more true than with a miscarriage. I had a conversation with a woman in her seventies who cried when she told me the story of her miscarriage. I felt comforted by her sadness, all those years later.

The bothersome thing about grief is that it rolls in, like a wave, and then rolls back out again. You never know when it's going to hit. Some days it just pooled around my feet. Some days it knocked me over, completely submerged.

The most inconvenient process.

My dear friend, Rickelle, lost her baby boy, Lake, when she was twenty-five weeks pregnant.

He was there. And then he was gone.

In the aftermath of such a trauma, Rickelle started planting in their backyard. She watered flowers, and she got a tiny orange kitten named Everett. She said, "I needed things to nurture. I longed for that baby; I was ready for him. So I needed something alive to take care of."

Rickelle wrote "I believe" on her hand every morning when she got out of bed. Between her kitten and garden caretaking, she went to the garage with a power sander and put a hoodie on and listened to reggae while she refinished furniture. This just goes to show you that you don't need to be reasonable when you are grieving.

She told me, "You just do whatever makes you feel an inch closer to putting one foot in front of the other."

I am in awe of people who have walked through this kind of grief.

I knew I hadn't lost a yolk sack. I knew I had lost a baby. The promise of what might have been. That's what I lost.

In the midst of the loss, we found out Steve was going to Bahrain, but the Stop Movement Order was still in effect. Luke, Lane, and I would be staying back in San Diego until we were allowed to join him. The general sentiment was that families would be allowed into Bahrain again, but the day Steve left, we had no idea when we would see him next.

"Take care of the kids," Steve whispered in my ear as we hugged goodbye, both of us just absolutely robotic from the weight of it all. He got into an orange cab in front of our rented house in Mission Hills. I had Luke in my arms as Lane slept upstairs. I was already pregnant again but didn't yet know it. Steve drove off and within a week I was trying to figure out a time when we could Skype so I could tell him the news.

Life wants to pull us into the next moment, the next moment, the next moment. Life wants us to turn the calendar page even when our souls want to stop and commemorate what is happening now. Life wants us to go to sleep and wake up and move on. The calendar is not conducive to our souls. The world is functioning in clock-time *chronos*, but our souls speak God-time *kairos*.

My instinct is to try to stay ahead of the grief, to march forward by the beat of chronos. I'm the kind of person who would rather "be strong" in the face of pain. I'd rather be "doing fine, thanks" than falling apart. But I've seen that the comfort does not come to those intent on coping. The comfort arrives for those who are willing to spill open.

Scripture says, "Blessed are those who mourn, for they will be comforted."[3] If we will allow ourselves the time and space to mourn, we will be comforted. On the other hand, if we believe we must suck it up and cope and steel ourselves against the loss, the comfort will be much harder to come by.

I learned from Rickelle that physically mourning—sanding, and watering, and digging, and feeding—blesses you with comfort. The act of letting go delivers gifts of comfort that marching on never will.

We allow a meal to be delivered. We allow a friend to sit quietly next to us. We allow God to touch us.

I am just now beginning to feel the weight of all these events. Dickinson was right on: my feet, mechanical, have gone round. Now, the cumulative effect of loss and change and uncertainty descend. My only charge is to let myself feel it all. To commemorate, and thereby let the comfort in.

I don't need to bow to chronos. The calendar will not serve me in matters of the soul. I don't need to assess how worthy or unworthy my losses are, how they do or don't stack up to someone else's plight.

My job is simply to allow myself to feel all these events—to let the crash happen—and not be in charge of forcing it all back together again.

First the chill, then the stupor, then the letting go.

16

chanting

Hope is the dream of a waking man.
—Aristotle

We got the news that we could join Steve in Bahrain. The ban on families had been lifted, and we were cleared to move.

Because Steve moved overseas two months before us, I was left to get our stuff packed up and get myself and the kids to the Middle East. The Navy (after some coaxing) finally allowed me to take a commercial flight—instead of a Navy flight—so I could bring a companion to help with the kids.

My life-saving friend Jamie agreed to accompany us and then stay a bit and help us get settled and just be a witness to the insanity of this entire proposition.

We flew from Ft. Lauderdale to Atlanta—uneventful.

We flew from Atlanta to Amsterdam—relatively uneventful. Jamie and Luke in the back of the plane. Lane and me in the middle of the plane. Both kids sprawled out for most of the overnight flight, digging their feet into the other person in the row (at one point, in her sleep, Lane put her foot on the man's shoulder next to her—"Um, excuse me. I'm sorry."). So between catnaps, Jamie and I tried to keep toddler limbs in check and keep toddlers from rolling off their makeshift beds, which only happened a couple of times in my case.

I took tiny little white pills the doctor had given me for pregnancy-induced nausea.

Then we got to Amsterdam. And the tone of the entire trip changed. "Your flight from Amsterdam to Bahrain is canceled."

"OK. What are our options?"

"You have no options. You will go to a hotel out in town tonight and come back for a 4:00 p.m. flight tomorrow."

"No, that's not going to work," I say to the woman, refusing to leave the counter. I knew I couldn't wrangle my children any longer than was already going to be necessary, and she had to get us on a flight. Somehow. Somewhere.

So she did. After fifteen minutes of vigorous typing and lots of Dutch and shaking her head and furrowing her brow and pursing her lips, she says . . .

"OK, I have a flight for you from here to Cairo and then Cairo to Bahrain."

"We'll take it."

I don't regret the decision now, knowing we're alive. But what followed was something equivalent to cheating death. And I'm not kidding.

Of course I didn't take into consideration we'd be two American women (one throwing up) flying with two small children into the heart of the Arab Spring on the eve of Ramadan. All I could see was getting to Bahrain, getting to my husband, and getting my children to their father. There was no other option.

We boarded EGYPTAIR—not particularly confidence-inspiring—and we headed to Cairo on what can only be described as the absolute most harrowing flight of my life. The turbulence was so bad that, at one point, I began screaming, "Dear God, please save us. Dear God, please save us. Dear God, please save us," as I clutched my children to me, who were both laughing at this point from the "wild ride, Mommy."

Because we were one of the last to get tickets on this flight, Jamie had to sit a dozen rows back and I had both the kids. Four hours of total chaos. People were throwing up. I was hysterical, literally sobbing after I finally stopped yelling. Passengers all around me were reaching out to me to hold my hand and give me a nod of reassurance, though none of us spoke the same language.

The flight attendant with the matte orange lipstick and heavy musk perfume even hugged me a couple of times.

The plane would drop and the engines would rev and then get very quiet and then the plane would drop and the engines would rev. No one ever said I was the calmest flyer in the world, but this was a fresh torture I had not known.

No one came on a loudspeaker to calm us. No one reassured us that the skies were just choppy that day. I felt like I was dangling in space—a ball of yarn being batted by the world's biggest cat paw—and we were on the absolute precipice of our death.

We finally landed in Cairo—two American women with strung-out children—and we tried to make our way through the crowds of Muslim men, hoping someone could help us locate the stroller so I could at least confine Luke and Lane.

A darkness and a heaviness met us in the Cairo airport. Groups of men sat on the floor in different corners of the airport. Talking adamantly, fingering prayer beads. We felt and looked like intruders stepping through and over their floor meetings.

We finally boarded our plane, and after another three hours or so, we landed safely in Bahrain. "It's so pretty," Lane said on our final approach—all the lights from the new financial harbor flickering in the very early morning darkness.

We landed at 3:00 a.m. with no luggage and no emotional reserves left. The relief was indescribable.

But the next morning Steve went back to work, and relief gave way to something much fiercer.

Panic.

Even with regular trips to the landmarks I loved, I felt panicked. The heat had not yet peaked, and with Ramadan in full swing, the options for entertaining my children were so incredibly and shockingly few. The heat intensified the smells of curry and body odor and my twelve-week-pregnant bloodhound sense of smell was offended at every turn.

When we checked in at the personal property office on base to let them know we had arrived and to schedule a dropoff of our belongings, we found out—through several visits and one particularly urgent conversation in which we were told that they had no record of our belongings coming to Bahrain whatsoever—that our belongings had been mistakenly put into storage in San Diego.

So it would be months, not weeks, before things like beds, dishes, toys, highchairs, and changing pads would arrive, since they had not yet left San Diego.

And then the news came about the seventeen SEALs killed in the Chinook shot down in Afghanistan. So many gorgeous young men lost. This, right after the siege on Bin Laden's compound. Such incredible highs and lows for one community to go through in such a short amount of time. We rode the tide of these events.

Jamie left.

"Madam friend all gone?" Anula, the Sri Lankan housekeeper, asks me in broken English.

"Yes, Anula. Madam friend all gone."

I took the kids to the child care on base, and I wrote an enormous check, and then I went back home and I got in bed and I cried.

I cried the kind of tears you cry when you're so very, very empty. When you're scared.

In the midst of this panicked sadness, the smallest miracle happened. One that I can't totally account for except to say that Christ saves us when we cannot save ourselves. Christ comes and sits with us when we cannot get ourselves up off the floor. The ways he saves us, the ways he keeps us company, are somewhat of a mystery. He arrives, and that's all I know.

This time, hope arrived on the wings of these words: "Things won't always feel the way they do right now."

And the ONLY thing that helped was saying over and over again—like a prayer, like a mantra, a chant—"Things won't always feel the way they do right now. . . . Things won't always feel the way they do right now. . . . Things won't always feel the way they do right now."

I just chose to believe that statement when I could believe little else. I chose to believe the scald I was feeling would let up at some point. I chose to believe that someway, somehow (though I didn't know when or how) it was all going to pass.

I wasn't in charge of anything other than the chanting. I would say it ritualistically to myself because I knew that if I could just hold a mantra in my head, the mantra would crowd out all the brain vultures vying for airtime, and the truth might be able to find its way from my head to my heart.

My job was to put the good words on repeat so the bad words couldn't compete.

Every time I began to feel the burn of the scald, I would say, "Things won't always feel the way they do right now." And somehow those words carried me through.

My friend Heather, from EA, talked a lot about her rituals. She said we all have rituals that help us get through our anxiety or our fear or our shame. Our rituals are what we use to cope, what we turn to for comfort when we start to feel the squeeze. Sometimes our rituals are healthy. Sometimes they are harmful. We choose ruin or we choose recovery.

I attached to this concept. I could see it in my own life. What do I do, where do I turn, on the down days. Or, as I've come to realize, the down hour—which is often butted up against some kind of moment of bliss only to have that gnawing settle in again.

Creating and turning to rituals that nourish us when we're experiencing a downturn is one of the ways we care for ourselves.

It was July when we arrived in Bahrain. It would be November before I felt a true lifting. It was four months—a third of a year—before things felt appreciably better, before I felt light again, before the panic floated away. It took *four* months. But it eased. It all eased.

Now, when I'm feeling the scald, I practice my chanting ritual. I know it will help bring my brain back to center.

One of the ways we can be there for ourselves like we would a friend is to be gentle when things are difficult. We chant our way through the panic instead of punishing. We wait for the panic to subside. We ask Christ to be our Company Keeper while we wait. Maybe nothing changes "out there," but having a strategy for coping with the panic can certainly change things "in here."

Going through such a huge transition can throw you into semi-hysterics at times. Or, let's be honest, even full-blown hysterics. Being without your belongings, receiving damaged household goods, figuring out how to do all the normals of life all over again (gas, groceries, hair, school, church, friends), caring for your family in the midst of your own disorientation . . . these are emotionally demanding tasks.

Some days can feel so incredibly inefficient that you just want to scream. *What have we done? How did we get here? Are we really starting all over . . . again?*

When navigating change, it's too easy for me to believe life will never feel right again, life will always feel as hard as it does in that very moment. This mindset keeps me stuck in perpetual hand-wringing, and I need a way to stop the toxic loop.

Hope is the wildness of possibility; it's the manifestation of resilience. When we're in the midst of a Come Apart, hope can feel fragile and fleeting, as though it will wing away if we move too quickly. This is the very time we need to hold onto hope the most, because hope always trumps hysterics.

Here's how I do it: "Things won't always feel the way they do right now."

On repeat.

17

going to the ganges

The problem with fantasy is the greatest benefit of fantasy:
it prevents us from living in the present moment.

—Geneen Roth

I decided to move our kids and myself to Bahrain because
we were allowed to go and because, when you're in the Navy,
sometimes you don't have the option to be together, so when
you do—even if it means uprooting—the Tanks choose to
pack up and go.

We were very low on glamour for pretty much our entire
tour in Bahrain. Just to give you an example: I gave Steve
bacon soap for Christmas the first Christmas we were there.

I mean.

I had wanted the exotic nature of this adventure to tran-
scend the logistics, and you know what, some days it sure
did. But most of all it was about creating a home on the

other side of the world, in an incredibly different culture, while mothering small children. It was about home, family, marriage. It was about building a small tribe we could rely on and cry and laugh with. It was about doing life together in a foreign place, which is both amazing and nuts.

I had so hoped for the glamour, but it peeked out very rarely. What we got, instead, was beauty-in-the-trenches. Some of you know what I'm talking about.

I liken our experience a bit to a story I read by Anne Lamott. She took a trip to India, and she had been waiting the entire trip to see the sunrise over the Ganges from a riverboat. A real dream of hers. But on the morning they went to the Ganges, the very last morning they were in India, the entire scene was socked in.

She writes:

> It was a thick, white pea-soup fog—a vichyssoise fog—and apparently we were not going to see any of the sights I'd assumed we would see, and in fact we had come here to see. But we saw something else: We saw how much better mystery shows up in fog, how much wilder and truer each holy moment is than any fantasy.[1]

You know what sucks? How true that is. Experiencing real beauty is about moving through the fogs of life and, also, allowing ourselves to be led when we can't see what we thought we'd be able to see.

Beauty and Hard hang out on the same side of town. But what if I want Glamour—the gal from trendy Uptown with the high messy bun and white teeth?

What happens when we chase the fantasy, when we long for the fantasy, and the fantasy doesn't deliver?

I don't know about you, but I usually self-medicate in some way or another. Actually, I do know about you. You self-medicate too. I know, I know, I'm such a downer. Calling us all out on our junkie MO. These are such inconvenient truths. We all find ways to deal with our internal worlds by manipulating and controlling and escaping through our external worlds.

A very soft and compassionate voice inside me says, "Do you know why you do this, Leeana? Do you know why everyone else does it too? Because you're trying to manage pain."

I believe the holy work is to look into the fog and see ourselves—scared, fragile, human—and take our pained self by the hand and lead him or her toward help. The holy work is not numbing ourselves into a fantasy, the happy-Edna-after thinking. The true, deep awakening is the beauty. Hard-won, blood-bath, horribly holy beauty.

Here's what I know: beauty often shows up best when the landscape is at its worst.

In other words, beauty is often that much more beautiful because things are so socked in.

I'll give you an example:

Weeks after we arrived in Bahrain, Jamie had left, and I was managing my panic, but I was not on easy street by any stretch. We were living in a temporary villa until we could move into our permanent one down the street. The landlord of the temporary villa called me one morning to see if a woman who might be interested in moving in after we left could come look at our place. Could I show her around?

"Sure," I told him. "I'm happy to show her the place."

An hour later, a woman showed up at my door. She was tall and had graceful gestures and a kind, if not ever-so-slightly tired, face. She had naturally curly brown hair and she had on white jeans, wedge sandals, and jade earrings and I was drawn to her immediately.

As I show her around the house, we realize our husbands work at the same command and one of her children is very close in age to Luke and Lane. She liked the house and wanted to bring her husband back to show him.

She came back with him and their three kids. And, after some negotiating and decision-making, she lets me know they're going to move into our place.

During all the back and forth, she and I talk more and I take a chance, risk appearing needy and glommy, and ask her if she'd like to get our kids together for a playdate sometime. They were new and we were new, and I figured we could all use some friends.

"Sounds great. Maybe after we get moved in and settled, we could get together," she says to me. They were still living in a hotel at the time.

"Of course. Yes, get settled and then let me know if that would work for you guys," I say.

We hang up and she calls me back twenty-five seconds later. A different tone in her voice.

"Leeana," she says, "I'm not sure why I just told you we should get settled before we get together. We could probably both use some support right now, so let's just make it happen. We're free tomorrow afternoon if you'd like to bring your kids to our hotel. Would that work for you?"

I don't even know that I had prayed for a friend. I just needed one. And God, in his grace, brought Jean to my front door. My. Front. Door. Christ came to me in the form of a friend, which is just grace. That's all.

The beauty of it was that much more beautiful, because it happened in Bahrain, where friends were few and troubles were many.

Jean was there when we had to limit all nonessential travel for the hundredth time and we needed some interruption to the boredom. We would get together and order food to be delivered and we'd make movie beds on the floor so our kids would have some fun in the midst of the world's tumult.

Jean was there when Luke swallowed the Bahraini coin and had to have an emergency endoscopy when Steve was out of the country. I sent Jean a text telling her I was at the hospital with Luke. She didn't ask me what I needed. She didn't tell me she would pray. She sent me a text that said, and I quote, "I'm on my way."

Most significantly, Jean was there when my beautiful baby Elle was born. She threw me a baby shower with little birds she hand-sewed and a garland of bubble-gum-pink fabrics and pink punch and pink tissue flowers hanging here and there. I can't emphasize how impossible it would be to pull something like this off in Bahrain, but she did it.

Jean knitted the hat Elle wore home from the hospital. She handmade gifts for Luke and Lane, too, and turned out to be one of the most thoughtful and generous souls I have ever known.

She was a witness when most everyone I knew was a world away, and what I couldn't get over, what I still can't get over, is that God brought her to my doorstep.

We wanted life to be the Ganges in all its glory. Turns out, some days the whole landscape is so socked in, you can't see from one moment to the next.

The work, the holy work, is to believe that somehow what is happening in that fog, that haze, that soup—if we will allow ourselves to sit in it and even invite Christ into it with us—is actually the whole point.

Marriages can be deeper because of the wounds they've survived and healed from.

Communities are closer because of the losses they've endured together.

Families learn to be a team because they rely on each other through seasons of change.

Friends trust each other through shared struggle and takeout.

I love fantasy. I love the feeling—whether through books or movies or music or clothes—of being transported to another time and place and way of thinking. But true living isn't fantasy.

True living is learning to tolerate the gifts in the mist.

We don't have to escape like we once did. We don't have to self-medicate like we once did. We aren't hurting as deeply and as severely as we once were. We aren't so desperate for the glamour. We can stand to be in the fog of the here, right now, in the present moment. We can open the front door and let the miracle in.

Wow, look at us!

18

saying no to the bad pants

She who does not find grace in herself dies slowly.
—Pablo Neruda

The other day I did something I should have never, ever done. I did something you should never, ever—under any circumstances—do.

In a moment of fear and worry and obsessive deficit thinking, I took a picture of my own butt.

I put on my raspberry all-purpose workout skirt that has the built-in raspberry spandex underneath. I lifted the back of the skirt up, held my phone behind me (shooting up toward my butt), switched the camera so that it was in mirror mode, and I clicked.

Then, I did the second dumbest thing I had done all day. I looked at the picture.

Of course, I was aghast. There, on my phone was an upward-facing shot of my own butt in tortured raspberry spandex. (Later, My Group told me this is the worst possible angle to shoot a butt and anyone who looks on Pinterest should have known that.)

I trashed it immediately for fear that I would accidentally, in some Freudian moment, post the picture to Instagram.

"Have you lost your mind?" Steve said when I told him what I did.

"Well, I just wanted to see what I was working with."

"And did that help?"

"No. No. IT. DID. NOT."

I got to thinking why taking that picture didn't help. I did get a good look at what I was working with. Too good a look, actually. The result wasn't motivating. It was misery.

It was me being my own bully.

It's the same conversation I've had with myself after I delivered babies. I would be so anxious to get out of my maternity jeans and into regular jeans that I would squeeze and contort and pour myself into ill-fitting pants just to be able to say to myself that I did it. What always, always ended up happening was my mood worsened and worsened as the day wore on and my body began swelling and oozing out of every seam.

May I give you an example:

Three months after Luke and Lane were born, I poured myself into pre-pregnancy jeans and felt like the world (and Steve) owed me some sort of gold star. I mentioned to Steve, as if I had done him some sort of favor, that I was in non-maternity jeans to which he said, and I quote, "OK."

"OK?!?!" I rip into him. "OK?!?! Did you hear what I just said? I had fifteen pounds of baby inside me three months ago, and I am now wearing non-maternity jeans. I think you should probably say something more than 'OK'!!"

"What do you want me to say," he continues digging, "I don't really get the big deal."

And then I did something I will blame on the fact that those pants were so tight they were cutting off oxygen to my brain.

I punched Steve in the ribs.

I don't mean I jokingly took a jab at him. I mean I punched him in the ribs.

I think we were both so shocked I actually hit him—hard—that we never spoke of it. We just stood there looking at each other and then we got in the car and ran our errands. Apparently those were tense times. Squeezy jeans were not helping matters.

Sometime after I had Elle I was sitting in traffic in my car with too-tight jeans on and felt, with such visceral disgust, my postpartum stomach observably expanding—like dough rising—out the top of these jeans. I said out loud after getting home and running upstairs to the safety and loyalty of my Zella yoga pants, "That's it. No more Bad Pants."

What I see, what catches me every time I've ever done this, as I'm peeling off the pants, is the red indentations all over my legs and stomach. Like a body that's been surgically scored. Isn't it amazing what we will do at our own expense.

I've decided that even if I have to wear something with a stretch waistband the rest of my life, I'm not going to demean myself by wearing clothes that hurt me. I'm just not going to do it anymore. The #1 criteria, for the very first time in my entire life, is no longer how something looks. The criteria is that it doesn't hurt me.

One of the ways we punish ourselves for not being more or better or thinner or stronger is by trying to squeeze ourselves—force ourselves, even—into all kinds of ill-fitting relationships. With other people, with ourselves, with our pants.

In our dysfunction, we spray-lacquer our clothing on, believing it will help us feel better. We only feel worse. Pinched. Squeezed. Restricted. Constricted. As we get well, we see that we no longer need to tolerate things that are hurting us (bad pants, bad boyfriends, bad friends, bad self-talk). We care about ourselves enough to stop confining ourselves. We care about ourselves enough to stop punishing ourselves.

All of these truths came rushing toward me after I took the picture of my own butt. I felt all those feelings of self-bullying, loathing, disgust, sadness, malice.

This is our junkie MO. Trying to find a fix that will satisfy us, like an addict. Trying to figure out the cocktail that will bring us the deep warmth and wholeness and belonging we crave. We'll wear pants that have to be painted on, even after we've had a baby and our bodies need to be mothered instead of murdered. We'll take pictures of our own butts. We'll sell ourselves out, time and time again, for the fix we think will—once and for all—help us feel safe in the world.

It never works. I will never take a good-enough Butt Picture. Ever. If my insides are hurting and untended, there isn't a Butt Picture in the universe that will make it all better. Not one. This is possibly the most profound truth I know.

If we are drowning in a void, everything we try to throw into that void will be consumed. Everything. Nothing will satisfy. Nothing will save.

I know this, and I forget this. I get panicked and scared and, instead of turning toward myself with compassion, I look for the fix. I grab the smallest pants in my closet and convince myself that if I can pour my body into them, I will feel whole again. The pants will satisfy the ache.

Nothing, even the best gifts God has given us, will satisfy the ache. The salvation is in our answer to that one little pesky question Christ is looking in my eyes and asking, "Leeana, do you want to get well?"

I take that question to be Christ's hand extended to me, reaching toward me in great love and grace, waiting for me to reach back and grab hold so he can pull me from the abyss.

The pants and the pictures and the pornography and the pills and the purging and the people-pleasing and the purchasing and the Pinot Grigio don't have that kind of power. Deep down, we know, but we also forget. If I'm ever going to be able to make changes in my life, I have to start with practicing radical love toward myself, not contempt. One tangible example is pants. I'm sure you can think of a dozen more.

I sit with myself as I would a friend instead of an enemy. I remind myself I'm not alone. I don't have to prove I'm worth something. I don't have to work to keep up with everyone's expectations of me. I don't have to live in order to avoid disappointing everyone who knows me. That's just crazy-making, soul-stealing. This kind of activity leaves us all exhausted, strung out, frantic for a fix.

I don't have to punish the less-than-pleasing parts of me. In fact, quite the opposite. I have to turn toward the less-than-pleasing parts of me, that annoying little shadow, with the most counterintuitive gesture. Radical grace; radical care.

I cannot deprive, punish, squeeze, or bully myself into feeling good enough. There aren't enough Bad Pants in the world to fill the void. There is only enough Christ.

So no more Bad Pants. No more Butt Pictures. Let's allow ourselves to breathe. Let's refuse to float out to sea on the waves of a thousand self-induced woundings. Let's stop restricting ourselves as a form of control or safety. Instead, every time we want to wear the Bad Pants, every time we want to take the Butt Picture, let's do ourselves a favor and ask what it is we really need. What am I really after here?

Can we offer ourselves what God has offered us, what the spacious people in our lives have offered us? Broad grace. A grace so large we can't find the end of it. So counter to the very small spaces we put ourselves in. So counter to the Bad Pants.

19

offering permission

Between stimulus and response there is a space. In that space is our power to choose our response. In our response lies our growth and our freedom.

—Viktor E. Frankl

At a certain point in my life, I began to require a strategy in order to shower. When it became necessary to take one (or more) children in the shower with me, I began weighing the importance of personal hygiene. *It's too hard. It's too much work. It doesn't really matter what I look like anyway.*

"You can get ready or you can go," my grandmother used to say. So I would just go.

Maybe, deep down, my ratty bun and yoga pants and my unconcealed eye-bags were a badge I wanted to show the world of how depleted things had gotten. Maybe, in some weird, twisted subconscious way, it felt good to look so bad because I needed others to see my secret struggle.

It's not entirely un-possible I liked looking like a victim.

Then one day, I started to get this gnawing feeling that I was constantly seeing my life as something that was happening to me, something to be managed, and the shower story became a microcosm of a bigger problem: my refusal to take personal responsibility for my life, my body, my health, my oily hair, my frantic way of being.

"This isn't a criticism, Leeana. It's merely an observation," my mom begins, "but what exactly is your plan with your hair?"

Lipgloss, showers, walks outdoors—these were now luxuries I just could not afford to make happen. *I just can't. I just can't. I just can't.* Everything was so acute and urgent internally that stopping, breathing, and applying the tiniest bit of makeup were just impossible tasks.

When it was time to pull things together, I could make it work. I could be as high functioning as needed, actually. But so little came from a place of ease or centeredness. My living—and this has been true of me for as long as I can remember—almost always originated out of a place of stress and striving. I rarely felt comfortable in my own skin.

C. S. Lewis writes, "I have said she had no face; but that meant she had a thousand faces."[1] As our souls are more and more depleted, we must keep up by taking on more and more faces. In the absence of our true self, we are a thousand different versions of who we were meant to be. This is exhausting.

Finally, it dawned on me: Why had I decided that this level of discomfort was an acceptable way to live? Even if I could control it all, even if I could manage the internal angst enough, why didn't I want more for myself?

Could I offer myself the permission to live out of something other than the "learned helplessness" our culture promotes with its endless options and scarcity mindset?

Could I offer myself the permission to live out of something other than stress?

The word *permission* is, in its origin, a "noun of action" in Latin. Permission can seem passive, an allowance or acquiescence. In reality, it's a conscious decision.

Offering permission is an act of personal responsibility. When life feels like it's happening to us, offering ourselves permission to do things differently is a way to live intentionally. We are paying homage to the fact that we always have options. We have, always available to us, a noun of action. For the longest time, the reality that I had options had completely slipped my mind.

We can offer ourselves permission to rest, to get help, to stop, to breathe. We can offer ourselves permission to pursue a passion, to dream, to forgive, to get on the treadmill. We don't have to wait. We can affect change.

Stress, chaos, urgency, and panic don't have to be what controls our lives. We actually have a say. We can allow ourselves the dignity of responding to our circumstances, even changing our circumstances, instead of just resigning to them.

Some of us are making the people around us miserable because we won't wake up and take personal responsibility for ourselves, our decisions, and our pain. We're defensive when we should be proactive. We're woeful when we could be whole. I don't know about you, but I want to be brave enough to get unstuck, to not hold my loved ones hostage by my inability to take personal responsibility for my wellness.

Growth and healing start by giving ourselves the permission to pursue them. If we aren't willing to show up and participate, then chances are, our souls will be lost on some level. And, chances are, it will affect the people who want to share life with us.

Was there a way I could take personal responsibility for my own well-being and decide I would not live in a perpetual state of inner stress anymore? Could I allow life to be good, enjoyed even, instead of always only managed?

Certainly, there are seasons in life when we must manage. But "managing" can become a habitual state of being, and the next thing you know, we are urgently living out of a perpetual deficit instead of taking the time to investigate what we really need, what we're really longing for.

It's scary to allow life to be good, especially if you've been through a lot of Hard. It's scary to let go of our worries and fears and resentments and anxieties and to celebrate the goodness that is now, that is here today. But, if we believe abundance is a trick and the bad thing is always just around the corner, then we will let the darkness win. Personally, I want to offer myself the permission to look for the light.

Christ gathers the crowds and his disciples and he asks the question that each of us must ask ourselves: "What good is it if you gain the whole world but lose your soul?"[2]

What good is it if we are playing the part, but inside, we are coming apart?

I told my friend Linsey I felt like there was a hole in the bottom of my bucket, like good things could come into my heart and soul, but there was this insidious drain that robbed me of really feeling the goodness. The drain, if I had to label it, was a triggered anxiety. My body could not shake it all out. The Hard piled on top of Hard, and I came to realize I was, at times, staving off panic.

I could feel I was adrift when I so desperately wanted to be awake. I could feel I was stuck—in this panicked paralysis—believing I was the victim.

Until I saw I had choices.

I believe there are many ways to be lost.

Lost in shame. Lost in fear. Lost in self-pity. Lost in self-sabotage. Lost in anger. Lost in food. Lost in substances. Lost in self-righteousness. Lost in promiscuity and false intimacy. Lost in our façades. Lost in people-pleasing. Lost in accumulation. Lost in deprivation. Lost in saving the world. A thousand faces, and no true face.

I have a friend who worked for a world-changing organization. She traveled the globe interceding on behalf of the poor, hungry, orphaned, marginalized. After months and months of relentless travel, she raised her hand, asking for a different pace. She loved the work; she simply needed a bit more downtime between trips. But the work had to move on. The organization had to push forward. The orphans and the widows had to be saved. Ultimately my friend wondered aloud if the orphans and widows were to be saved at the expense of her own soul, her own marriage, her own health. When the organization maintained that the world couldn't wait for her to recover, she left the job.

Years later, innumerable treatments later, her body is still traumatized from that work. When she left, everyone thought she was nuts. How could you leave *that* organization, *that* job, *that* kind of global influence?

She said, "There has to be a different way. I cannot be the collateral damage in God's vision for the world."

In other words, what good is it to gain the whole world but lose my one and only soul?

She gave herself the permission to choose herself. Instead of allowing her entire life to be victimized by the job, she took personal responsibility and reclaimed her own soul.

Did people stand up and applaud that decision like they did when she was traveling the globe? No. She didn't get awards and honors for resting. What she got, instead, was a truer, healthier version of herself. For some people, that trade-off isn't worth it. Personally, I don't believe living with a lost soul is worth it. Ever. There is no trade-off that will justify bartering our souls.

I believe I am a person who will probably always fight this low-lying stress, the anxiousness. I am someone who will probably always need some measure of help to keep myself centered, to keep that hole in the bottom of the bucket securely plugged and no longer robbing me of the abundance and gratitude.

My job is to give myself permission for all that to be OK.

In the book of Luke, Jesus tells a trilogy of parables about being lost. The Pharisees are up in his face about eating and drinking with sinners. *Why are you hanging out with that crowd, Jesus? They're no good. They're riffraff.* Jesus rebuts their accusations by telling three stories: the story of the woman who lost her coin, the story of the lost sheep, and the story of the prodigal son.

In each parable, the emphasis is on the urgency of finding even one who is lost and the celebration when what was lost has been found.

I think about the courage of the prodigal son. He is with the pigs, out of cash, out of options. Sitting in the sty, he must offer himself the permission to return to his father's house. He could have let pride stand in his way. He could have let his own shame keep him from his father's love. He could have let the inertia of his own decisions keep him stuck and, therefore, lost. He didn't.

He realized he needed to start walking. And he let himself do it.

Soon, he sees his father down the path, running toward him.

Butcher the fattened calf! My precious child has come home!

Lost is met head-on by Love.

These days, I'm offering myself the permission to take a step toward home—the place where my true self meets God's presence. Fumbling and stumbling my way there, if I must, offering myself permission to nurture the one and only soul God has given me.

We are both lost and found. And no matter where we are on the road home, we are loved. That's it. Can we, with our one true face, look into the eyes of Love and bear the light of his glory and grace.

20

channeling your inner navy SEAL

Fear doesn't go away. The warrior and the artist live by the same code of necessity, which dictates that the battle must be fought anew every day.

—Steven Pressfield

My husband has been in the SEAL teams for sixteen years. Over the ten years Steve and I have been married, I've heard great stories about his job. My very favorite, though, is a story from his days as a BUD/S student.[1]

During the infamous "Hell Week," the guys are intentionally sleep deprived and then made to accomplish physical tasks, usually in some form of competition. At any time during this week, any SEAL candidate can go to the large bell on the shore and ring it if they'd like to be removed from training. No one is forced to do anything. You can quit at any time.

One evening, late into "Hell Week," the instructors told the students to get their boats and head out into the ocean. They needed to paddle to a specific buoy, loop around it, and then paddle back to the shore. As the officer in his boat, Steve was given the task of calling out commands to the rest of the guys onboard.

They headed out into the surf, and after they had been underway for a bit, Steve calls to his crew, "Around the gate. Around the gate!"

"Sir," one of his crew members points out, "there is no gate."

"Around the gate!" Steve insists. "Around the gate!"

"Sir," the crew member maintains, "we're in the middle of the ocean. *There is no gate.*"

Suddenly Steve realizes his sleep-deprived eyes are creating a mirage in the middle of the ocean. "Yes, yes," he changes commands, "continue straight ahead."

And they paddle on.

I love this story for two reasons: First, it's funny to imagine my husband so tired he's seriously telling a team of men to paddle a boat around a gate in the middle of the Pacific Ocean. Second, it beautifully illustrates how easy it is for us to get so worn down that all we perceive are the impediments.

For me, I feel better and I do better if I can get a bit of writing done on a consistent basis. It's like soul yoga for me—centering and calming and a way for me to process my world. Things feel much more chaotic when I don't release some energy through written words.

However, my life is not really conducive to this kind of thing. My life is, at any given moment, in some form of overstimulation. In fact, just today, in order to create room on my desk for my laptop, I had to move piles of preschool artwork, a wire basket of unidentified paperwork, a roll of camouflage Duck Tape, a Target bag full of returns, diaper rash cream, and three empty Coke Zero cans. In order to even get to my desk, I had to wend my way through the gauntlet of two full laundry baskets, two empty rifle cases, a ground pad, and a Pack 'n Play. This is just what it takes. These are the real or perceived impediments to getting a bit of soulwork done each day. My husband's needs. My kids' needs. Our family's needs. Piles of stuff. All weighed out against my own needs. How do I figure out the balance?

"The only easy day was yesterday," the guys say to each other in training. In other words, don't expect things to go smoothly. In fact, the truth is, things are about to get crazy up in here.

Some of us are trying to do some pretty big things in life: raise kids, earn a degree, hone a craft, change our relationship with food, stay married, become less codependent, recover from trauma, connect with our more intuitive self, launch a business, save the world.

When we're trying to lean into life, it's very easy for impediments to present themselves out of thin air, telling us we must change course, or even abandon ship.

Some of us have become so tired and so sensitized that when an impediment shows itself—again, real or perceived—we're done. We avoid stepping into the fray of life for fear of failure. We let anxiety convince us that we can't manage difficult things. We choose to numb instead of engage. Soon we begin believing we're not capable of handling the challenges life brings.

Perhaps it's time to channel our inner Navy SEAL and get back in the game. Some days we need to sit down and rest. Some days we need to get up and fight!

Often, I must clear out a path to my soulwork. It's never easy, but it's always worth it. Always. I have every excuse in the book to quit, but I know that quitting is not going to serve me.

Some of us have tried and failed so many times we have lost trust in ourselves. One of the ways we build that trust back is by making manageable commitments to ourselves and following through. More than just accomplishment, the follow-through sends the message we're worth fighting for, our projects matter, and our contribution to the world counts.

In BUD/S, Steve tells me you just focus on getting to the next meal. You don't think about making it through the day or the week or the entire training schedule. If you think that way, you'll quit. You just try to make it to the next meal.

When it comes to accomplishing something that matters, you usually can't sit down in one weekend and manically get the whole thing done. You have to work in manageable chunks and, over time, you see that you've really gotten somewhere. You don't typically make significant progress in life in frantic bursts. Instead, I think life seems to reward resolve.

This is both the great pain and the great beauty of participating in an endeavor that requires sustained time, energy, and stamina. We can't complete it on a whim. We can't go to one meeting and declare ourselves sober. We can't paint for one morning and consider ourselves an artist. We don't have a great business idea and immediately become an entrepreneur.

We must make commitments and follow through. I believe the long haul matures us, offers us valuable lessons that come through our sustained participation in a process.

So many of us have believed that being a friend to ourselves meant allowing ourselves to languish in self-pity and anxiety so we never had to get anything done again. We saw this as a way we took care of ourselves: never expected anything difficult of ourselves again. We believed no participation in life was better than imperfect participation, and now we're ever-so-slightly flatlined.

If we made a commitment to a friend, we would do our best to make good on it. We would honor what we set out to do because we care about our relationship with that person. We treat ourselves badly when we make commitments to ourselves that we don't honor. Or, we refuse to make commitments to ourselves because we are convinced we won't be able to accomplish our goal anyway. We give up before we've begun.

When we do this, we're sending the message to ourselves that we don't actually value what we're working on and it doesn't really matter that much anyway. Or, fatalistically, that no matter what we do or try, it won't make any difference. So, why not be flakey. Why not check out. Why not be OK with quitting.

We've self-sabotaged so many times we've lost trust in ourselves. Making one small manageable commitment and following through can be an olive branch we extend to ourselves and a foundation from which to build, a way we get back in touch with our own inner strength.

Are you working on something big? Needing some momentum or traction? Why not start with one small, manageable commitment. Something you know you can get done. And then follow through. Do it. And then celebrate the doing of it.

You made it to the next meal? You painted for a half hour this morning? You took the baby out for a walk? You wrote that difficult email? You embraced your body instead of punishing it today? You finally planted those herbs? You filled out the paperwork? You made something with your own two hands? Congratulations! You've got a little momentum to work off of. And that's really something!

One of the things that gets all tangled up in this making a commitment to ourselves and following-through business is our fear.

What if it doesn't turn out perfectly?
What if I fail?
What if no one notices?
What if it's hard?
What if I don't have any support?
What if people don't get it?
What if I suck?
What if _____ could do it better?
What if I work so so so hard and it doesn't end up
*   mattering anyway?*
What if I'm disappointed?
What if I end up with regrets?
What if . . . ?

I rehearse these "what-ifs" all the time.

What if I work for years and it never amounts to
*   anything?*
What if no one gets it?
What if I'm running out of time?
What if she beats me to it?
What if I'm just an amateur?
What if it's too hard?

These are the days when I'm stuck in my own closed loop, believing (erroneously) that life is only all about the product, when I have come to realize that life is actually so much more about the process.

158

Entering into the process is nearly always a mess. We will never be able to do things perfectly and glamorously all the time. *Tragic, I know*. What we're talking about here is walking into the mess and trusting that the process itself has great gifts to offer if we will get up off the couch and participate.

Life is going to hand us Hard over and over again. Here's what you and I can do:

> You make a pact with yourself, something manageable. And you keep that pact. You firmly treat yourself with gentleness. That's the key. You love yourself too much to let yourself fade away. You channel that inner Navy SEAL and you tape the following mantra to your bathroom mirror: "The Only Easy Day Was Yesterday" and then you go get to work.
>
> You do this because you care about being alive and awake in the world, about being conscious, about inhabiting your own life. You do this because you want to make some kind of small or large contribution, because you want to be whole.
>
> You do this as a way to honor your true self.

Not out of anxious striving but out of a deeper calling, you peck away. A tiny bit at a time. For the long haul. You are unwilling to live with an untold story. You are unwilling to silence your one and only voice.

Over time, you will look back at the body of work you've created, or the personal growth you've experienced, or the memories you've made with your children, or the connection you feel with your partner, or the incremental progress you've made professionally, and you'll see that these small commitments and your follow-through have actually added up. Somehow, that inner Navy SEAL was able to rescue your hostage self from the captors of shame and fear and anxiety and self-pity.

Hooyah!

Just shows you what you can do when you lean into the Hard, when you get in touch with that warrior within.

We learn to believe in ourselves again when we face challenges with courage. We will not conquer everything in our path. We may not have perfect abs while going into battle, but we can still fight. We can still push up against life a bit. We can still show up. We can still arise and put on our war paint!

Hey, life, I'm here. I'm not going to let you beat me. I'm not going to drift out to sea. Period. Even if the only easy day was yesterday. Bring. It. On.

And if it all goes sideways (because it will, at some point), I will take a nap or a hot shower and then I will come for you again. I will begin again. I will put on the war paint AGAIN. Hear me roar.

I'm not sure what you're working on today. Perhaps you're working on a creative project, realizing a dream, getting/ staying sober, or surviving a divorce. Maybe you're working on grief today because grief is like a job sometimes. Maybe you're working on a new business venture, home school curriculum, a big decision, a friendship, a vegetable garden, or getting your baby to sleep through the night. Maybe you've just moved or maybe you're barely moving.

Whatever you want to get accomplished today, here's to channeling your inner Navy SEAL. Sometimes in life the only easy day was yesterday. And yet, I believe we honor ourselves by getting to work even when—especially when—the opposition is rising up out of thin air.

Around the gate, dear friends. Around the gate!

21

jiggling

We do not think ourselves into new ways of living, we
live ourselves into new ways of thinking.

—Richard Rohr

When you have small children and live overseas and have
flown around the world with these small children and have a
Type A husband, you might (*you know, just a thought*) need
to check on your mental health.

You might need to be sure that you aren't turning into the
woman in Charlotte Perkins Gilman's "The Yellow Wallpaper" who began peeling the wallpaper from her attic bedroom
asylum because she felt as though the pattern had turned into
bars that were caging her in. Not that any of us have ever felt
that way, of course, ever.

The truth is, when things are Hard, sometimes the angst
can become a companion and we forget how to be happy.
We are so used to sitting with the melancholy that we forget

how to live, how to function, without it. We lose our sense of humor. We lose our ability to let loose.

When I need to help my mind, my mind is the problem, so it's not readily offering me any real solid solutions. A trick I've learned is to begin with my body. What's something I could do for my body right now that would help my mind? In other words, if I do something different with my body—often something nurturing or caretaking or invigorating—the goodness penetrates.

If I want to get especially wild, I go outside.

The Come Apart whispers in our ear that we don't have the energy to do much of anything, much less get ourselves out the door. But time and time again I have seen that when natural elements touch my body—water, sun, air, dirt, grass, breeze—that organic matter reaches through my skin and relief arrives in my heart and mind.

Additionally, making this small decision to take care of ourselves always makes a difference. Our kindness to ourselves does not return void. The companionship unlocks a softer side, and we find we don't have to be as uptight, stressed, or worried as we thought we did.

Halfway through our tour in Bahrain, we came back to the States to visit family, introduce Elle around, and take a break from the Middle Eastern summer. We traveled around the world with two three-year-olds and a four-month-old. Apparently we were pretty desperate for that break.

On the last leg of our trip, we met Steve's family at Boyne Mountain, Michigan, and we all stayed right on Deer Lake.

After the Bahrain beige, I felt as though I had never actually seen the color green before when we drove through the tunnel of trees on our way to the lake. I had never seen red before like I saw it on the old barn. I had never smelled air so damp and fresh. I had never seen a thunderstorm over a lake. I felt as though scales were coming off my eyes, a layer of armor falling from my skin.

We took Uncle Paul's whaler out for a turn on the lake and Steve hooked up a huge inner tube to the back. I jumped in, gave him the thumbs up, and I was immediately whipping around the choppy water, laughing my head off.

Lane cheered me on from the boat while, back on shore, Elle napped and Luke played with Grammie.

Somehow in this magic moment, all the kids were accounted for and I was skimming off the water in a huge inner tube—postpartum body jiggling like a jello salad—giggling and giggling and giggling. It was like a match was struck and a candle was lit in my heart. Warm, white light. A vigil for all things whimsical.

When life becomes like a too-tight belt, a stuffy suit, a girdle, do me a favor: take a ride on an inner tube. Turn on the sprinklers in the front yard and run. Let your body jiggle a bit. Laugh your head off. It's like life will begin again.

I couldn't believe how good it felt to just let go. We had spent a year being vigilant, and that had made us a much more serious version of ourselves. Jiggling across Deer Lake was the antidote to releasing my grip on Hard.

A couple days later, a storm came in. Once the lightning and thunder passed, Steve thought it would be a great idea to head out onto the lake in the whaler. In the driving rain. *Sure! Why not.*

Of course, Luke and Lane weren't going to be left behind. Neither was cousin Fynn. So Steve and I hoisted the kids up and waded out to the boat, threw the kids in, and jumped aboard.

We raced around that lake with the rain hitting our faces like ice chips. You know that feeling? And we were all just completely soaked despite a few pieces of tried-and-true REI gear. I clutched both my getting-big kids on my lap—one on each knee—proud of their adventurous spirit. Steve skimmed us over the water and we screamed and pulled our hoods down as best we could.

Too often I can't will myself out of my own head. I'm stuck in the smallness of my own mind. But if I will think about what my body needs—even while my mind is wild and frantic and playing all kinds of tricks on me—and follow through on that physical need, the emotional and mental tangle somehow slackens and I can begin pulling the knots loose.

Some of us have gone through sensitizing events that have left raw nerves exposed. From there, even after time and healing, we have a hard time completely letting go. We find that our fists are clenched and our breath is caught because we're waiting . . . waiting . . . waiting for that other shoe to drop, for the bottom to fall out, for the sky to come crashing down. Even if we don't fully realize it, we are perpetually anticipating a mess.

Part of this is because we have been through a mess, and so it follows—somewhere down deep inside us—that the mess is always just around that next corner or always at our backs. Threatening us. Ready to dissolve all that we cherish.

We steel ourselves, prepare for the letdown, rehearse the melancholy. All in an attempt to avoid being blindsided, I think.

I'm a gifted hand-wringer and white-knuckler. Especially in this last handful of years. I got so serious, almost lost my sense of humor altogether at times. Laughter is one of those very few things that helps our brains and our bodies deal. Laughter helps us melt, makes us pliable, where we were once so rigid.

Not yet six months back from our tour in Bahrain, Steve and I celebrated our tenth wedding anniversary. We drove from San Diego up to the heaven-on-earth Northern California cities of Monterey and Carmel.

We went to Asilomar to follow the coastline walking trail. I looked out over the very beach where, three years prior, I had confessed to the trees that I wished everyone would just leave me alone.

We walked from Asilomar to the Lone Cypress, following the rugged coastline. The rolling, misting fog. The sea spray. The restless, churning water. Steve scampered from our path down to the tide pools to investigate. I wore my super-soft Charger shirt and drank my Americano as slowly as I could.

Tissue-weight cotton on my shoulders. Pink-cheek chill on my face. Damp beach air in my lungs. The smell of espresso and ocean in my nose. The chemicals in my body shifting from the endorphins.

Space. And, with each step, a bit more space.

Around each bend of the coastline was more to see, more to inhale. The beauty just did not end. I felt like my brain had been newly washed and a capacity created for joy.

At one point, we looked down from the trail onto the sand and there, fashioned out of rocks by a previous beachgoer, were the words THANK Y♥U.

Oh God of espresso, God of smooth sea stones, God of ten years together, thank you for a heart of flesh. Thank you for not leaving me alone, even when I asked you to.

22

practicing plenty

Whoever you are, you are human. Wherever you are, you live in the world, which is just waiting for you to notice the holiness in it.

—Barbara Brown Taylor

Throughout our time in Bahrain, the Sunni and Shi'a infighting limited our movement and liberties. Additionally, with the attacks on the United States Embassies in Libya and Cairo, and the aftermath of the Jones's anti-Muslim video, we were often asked to stop any nonessential travel.

The island of Bahrain is very small. My children were very small. Add liberty restrictions to an already restricted life, and you have what can begin to feel like a postage-stamp worth of emotional space.

Many other women seemed to manage this all beautifully, with exotic vacations to neighboring countries and the most gorgeous pictures you have ever seen on Facebook. We found beautiful moments in the midst of "The Troubles," but it was not with the ease that others seemed to be experiencing their life in Bahrain.

At a particularly aggressive point in the civil infighting, our friends threw a wine tasting party. Because everyone bought their wine, beer, and liquor from the tiny, two-aisle package store on base, everyone had the exact same bottles as everyone else.

Then, every so often, a row of tables would be set up in the Exchange and there would be what the signage referred to as a "Wine Event." This meant you could taste and purchase wine—different bottles than what were usually carried in stock—and you didn't have to use your alcohol ration points.

Our friends had the brilliant idea of asking the purveyors of this special event if they wanted to do an in-home party and bring some of their wine for tasting. If people wanted to buy, we would write down our names and the bottle(s) we wanted and then we'd have to go pay and pick up our bottles at the Exchange the next morning.

This is a perfect example of how our lives were much more monitored and institutionalized in Bahrain, mainly due to safety concerns. What we could wear, how much alcohol we could purchase (and when and where we could purchase it), where we could go, what we could say to whom—aspects of our lives were censored in ways they don't need to be in other settings.

So our friends wanted to throw a wine tasting party! At their house, a thick-accented Italian woman opened a few bottles, told us about each of them. Acidic, earthy, jammy, bright. We were all relaxing, enjoying something different, euphoric from the freedom we were feeling inside the walls of their villa.

Then, like the opening scene from *Navy SEALs*, the guys' phones started to ring. First one. Then another. Then another. Each one getting called into work. Within ten minutes, just about every male at the party, including our host, disappeared from the crowd.

As the door opened and closed and the guys exited, one about every minute at this point, an acrid smell filled the courtyard of the villa and blew into the entryway.

Every mucus membrane on your face immediately acknowledged our new party guest:

Tear gas, blowing over from a nearby riot.

This was Bahrain. Earnest attempts to throw a party and preserve some kind of normalcy, or our version of normalcy, that usually ended up awash in tear gas. You had to laugh.

You just never knew exactly how your life was going to be interrupted, but you knew it was going to happen. Make plans to go to the mall and be sure a pipe bomb was found in the parking garage that day. Decide to go to the Shi'a village for pottery, and prepare for roadblocks and tire fires. Try to get your kids to school, and get ready to witness burning dumpsters, riot police, and angry graffiti.

To be honest, I felt stuck so many times. In order to leave the island, I would have to get on a plane with three small children. I couldn't travel freely on the island because of infighting. The weather and traffic seemed to be constantly pushing against me.

This is what people often forget about adventures. They are exciting, and they are hard. Especially challenging when you have decided to bring your entire family along for the ride.

Jean and I were often together and we would buoy each other when things seemed most dire. We'd decided that being in the adventure together was going to be much, much better than being in it alone.

Shortly after the wine tasting party fiasco, I walked into Jean's kitchen one afternoon and saw a cookbook on her counter that I hadn't seen before. Jean always had gorgeous cookbooks with sensual pictures. She'd drive thirty minutes out of her way to find the best produce for her creations. That was one of her portals, I think. Putting a beautiful meal on the table was her rebellion against a reality that wasn't always easy. Creating gorgeous food expanded her life.

For our Christmas gathering, Jean made white bean hummus—creamy and garlicky—garnished with thin ribbons of basil, effortlessly formed into an abstract shape of a Christmas tree. Little pomegranate seeds sprinkled here and there looked like bulbs on the branches. I literally cried when I saw the white bean hummus with the basil Christmas tree. Cried.

The cookbook in Jean's kitchen was thick and hardback, a stark white background on the cover punctuated with two halves of a roasted eggplant. The title, written in all caps across the middle of the book, was *PLENTY.*

This was a word I did not feel, and yet, it was the word I longed for.

Jean's cookbook was a banner reminding me to practice PLENTY. Even when there seemed to be little. Even when it felt like the resources were going to run out. Even when the region was volatile and we felt in the dark so much of the time. Even when there was no good lettuce at any store, anywhere. Even when the wind carried tear gas.

We could find plenty.

Instead of needing everything on the outside to change in order to feel "good," we saw that we could find within ourselves a *posture of plenty* even if we weren't necessarily experiencing a *place of plenty*.

This is where the rugs come in. Jean and I needed something beautiful to look at, something that would expand our life without us having to pick up and go anywhere.

The rugs became our shared portal.

Some nights, we'd get all our kids tucked in and we'd escape our homes together and drive straight for Shawarma Alley to a rug shop Jean introduced me to.

When we lived in Bahrain previously, I had loved going to Yousef's shop in the souq, but the souq was rarely accessible this time around so we needed a shop closer to our homes in Juffair. Mr. Mohammed's Carpet House was just the shop. Jean and I would have tea with Mr. Mohammed and run our bare feet across anything new he had to show us, sometimes shopping, sometimes just admiring.

For New Year's Eve, we decided we wanted one last party in our villa before the movers came. We asked Mr. Mohammed if he would come put on a rug flop at our house, a traditional Middle Eastern party where a rug dealer brings hundreds of rugs to your house and flops them while you and your guests enjoy local food.

Mr. Mohammed filled our dining room table with shawarma, tabouli, hummus, naan, tikka. And he filled our entryway with rugs from all over the region. Qum. Qashqai. Kashkuli. Nain. Tabriz. Kashmir. Tribal carpets. Kilims. City carpets. Wool. Silk.

Mr. Mohammed flopped rugs for hours, one on top of another, calling out their region, materials, price, size, quality.

Every rug that hit the next would give off a billow of sand, filling our entire downstairs with ancient smells.

We rang in the New Year with new friends while we haggled for rugs right there in our Middle Eastern living room.

Mr. Mohammed gave me a small square tribal rug from Baluchistan that sits in front of my closet. I walk on that rug a million times every day, and I never set foot on it that I don't think about how the rugs were part of my salvation.

They were the broad place, the endless beauty, the expanse, when many other things felt small. They were magic carpets that flew me to a different land or, maybe more accurately, showed me the beauty right where I was.

We lived two doors down from a small, neighborhood mosque, and every Friday at noon, when the mosque was at its fullest, the prayer rugs would spill out into the streets and our unpaved roads were covered with carpets. The men would leave their rugs in the street and head to lunch, and I snapped picture after picture of the juxtaposition of these elaborate rugs, pinks and reds atop the sandy street, cars driving right over them.

Sometimes life lacks space, and we have to find the portals that will take us to larger moments, grandeur. The portals remind us of the resilience and artistry of the human spirit. They are reminders of the plenty.

Tear gas is always going to be part of life. Choking and sputtering on the clouds of violence and dissonance and hatred. Division, war, plague, grief, infighting. Is it possible that a tiny wrinkle in time could present itself, a wormhole or a looking glass through which we might see a kind of majesty that expands our senses?

Plenty means "fullness," an invitation to see our circumstances as more than just one-dimensional. Whether we're stuck on the floor with small children, stuck in a job we don't love, stuck in a bed from illness, stuck in the house in a foreign country while tires burn outside, we can still find fullness—though it might not be evident at first glance.

We are not without.

There is plenty of love. Plenty of hope. Plenty of friendship. Plenty of creativity. Plenty of laughter. Plenty of time. Plenty of beauty. Even one friend is plenty, if we learn to do life together.

Life offers us so much more than *enough*. We have, at our fingertips, *plenty*. The most revolutionary thing we can do is choose to see the fullness instead of the lack, no matter where life has us.

We look for the portals. Not as an escape, but as a reminder of his kingdom come. As a posture of plenty.

23

wandering like
a gypsy

The ragamuffin who sees his life as a voyage of discovery and runs the risk of failure has a better feel for faithfulness than the timid man who hides behind the law and never finds out who he is at all.

—Brennan Manning

I didn't realize Elle wouldn't like grass. All kids like grass, right? But when I sat her down on grass for the first time in her life, she cried and tried to pick her legs up so she wouldn't get poked. She was almost one when we returned to the States from Bahrain and she'd never been put down on grass. The green blades were foreign, an assault on her chubby baby thighs.

What a metaphor for transition. Something as lush as grass, when never experienced, is simply strange, even aggressive.

When you start over, you have to start over. Those are the rules. In your new environment, there's so much to take in, so many new things to adjust to. With all the adjusting and learning and beginning again, life can feel like perpetual wandering.

But, the truth is, whether you live like we do and you move around quite a bit, or you live in the same house thirty years, life rarely arrives in the ways you think it's going to. So we might as well make peace with the wandering.

My goal is to be like the gypsies. Roam. Stop and eat. Dance. Roam. Stop and eat. Dance. Wouldn't that be a lot more fulfilling than trying to choke some preconceived destination out of life. What if I could circle the wagons, no matter where I find myself, and put on a great party?

Someone said to me recently that the wandering isn't futile. There's an intention to it, a drilling down with each pass we make, deeper into ourselves, deeper into our stories, deeper into the heart of Christ, deeper into the arms of each other.

I have a friend who suffers from chronic health issues and has for years. So much of her life she has felt sidelined because her body has played terrible tricks on her, abandoned her over and over again. She has been an incredible advocate for herself, pursuing all kinds of treatments, care, ideologies, philosophies, practices, and approaches. While she is incrementally better at this writing, she is not healed.

Recently, a stranger told her—in a somewhat prophetic moment—that he knew she felt like she was watching life from the sidelines.

"Instead of being on the bench," he says, "you are actually on a bridge. Though it feels like you're getting nowhere, you're on a very important path—a passage that leads from something to something."

The problem is, as Ecclesiastes 3 points out, we don't always know what God is doing from beginning to end. And though we are told he is making things beautiful in its time, the whole plan is a bit mysterious, isn't it.

I thought this image of the bridge was particularly helpful. We can feel like we're on the bench, but the truth is—even if we don't realize it—our wandering does produce. What it produces, and when the production will happen, well, that is all out of our hands, which is the very bad news.

Our job is to trust that the journey matters.

This same friend recently reminded me of the story of Naaman, a rich and powerful warrior in the Old Testament who fell ill with leprosy.[1] Naaman goes to the prophet Elisha for healing, and Elisha sends a servant girl out to tell Naaman to go wash in the Jordan seven times and his skin will be healed.

Naaman is furious. Why does Elisha send a child messenger to tell him he must go wash in the most filthy water in Israel? *Come on. This can't be the plan. Doesn't Elisha know who I am? I don't take instructions from children. And I definitely don't do the Jordan.*

Ultimately, Naaman's servants convince him to just give it a try. *Is it possible, Naaman, that this just might work? Can you give up control and just try?* So he goes to the Jordan and dips his body in seven times.

I'm sure Naaman thought, as he's dunking his body in the nastiness of the Jordan—three, four, five—*This is insane. Why am I here? What am I doing? This makes absolutely no sense. There has to be a much more glamorous way than* this.

Reluctantly, he obeys, and he emerges from the water healed. The NIV says his skin became like that of a young boy, which makes me laugh. Naaman thought he was going to the barfy Jordan, but God was actually leading him to the fountain of youth. Isn't that like God to use the gross for his glory and shut up the whiner.

I don't like to wander any more than Naaman liked dipping himself in the Jordan seven times. I'm sure that felt incredibly counterintuitive to him. Crazy, even. But sometimes we aren't the ones with the master plan. Scratch that. We are never the ones with the master plan. We must focus our attention on Tolkien's perfect line that says, "All who wander are not lost."

True beauty, healing, is found in the most unlikely places, and richness of soul does not typically come to us in the times when we are feeling perfectly at ease. Haven't you seen that to be true in your own life?

Not arriving can be so painful. Waiting can be so painful. That seeming lack of progress. The feeling that we're not getting anywhere. But it's in the wandering that we pick up new truths, stumble across new paths, acquire unforeseen knowledge, link up with companions and guides.

How difficult it is for us to accept the labyrinth of life. We journey into the depths of ourselves only to journey back out again. This is an indirect practice. Never perfectly efficient. Like the labyrinth, our stories are meandering and yet purposeful. The journey contains great significance. But, can we accept circuitousness? Or do we internalize indirectness as a failure?

What if we could embrace the gypsy within and accept—celebrate even—the journeying, the non-arrival of life? How might our anxiety levels and our toxic thinking change if we were to see ourselves as experiencers and not require ourselves to be experts? How might we be inspired to risk courageously, love generously, live expectantly if we could accept the journey?

Sometimes it's OK to just not know, to not know the end from the beginning, to not understand how we're going to get there from here.

Being a companion to ourselves means we don't have to fix it or figure it out. Instead, we can flex. Take the next step. More will be revealed. We can pray for God to help us tolerate the waiting and the seeming lack of control, to help us focus on what we can control, which is how we treat ourselves in the middle of the uncertainty.

It takes courage to not know the destination and to still participate in the journey. Even bratty Naaman had the courage to try. *Oh, well, what do I have to lose? After all, I can sit in my house and die of leprosy or I can go to the Jordan. At this point, what's the worst thing that can happen?*

The word *courage* comes from the Latin word *cor*, meaning "heart." To be courageous, then, means to be people of the heart. Not people of the white-knuckling, glamour-seeking, must-be-perfect, I'm-too-good-to-wander world. Not people of control.

People of the heart.

I believe we all want to be people of the heart. We don't want to be marking time, living in survival mode for any longer than is absolutely necessary at times. We don't want to eke life out. We want to flourish.

This requires courage.

It takes courage to make one small step in the right direction, especially when we don't know the exact destination. When we take that next right step, our one part courage is met with a thousand parts God's grace. And we can make a long journey that way. We can move through life that way. We can find freedom that way. One small step at a time. One dunk in the Jordan at a time.

Emily Dickinson wrote, "The Truth must dazzle gradually / or every man be blind."[2] God does not send us the entire story up front. If he did, we'd be blind. The way of God is a gradual dazzling, an unfolding. He brings us along with small miracles, saves us in bits, rescues us one little lightbulb at a time.

Our job is not to figure out the whole path. Our job is to take the very next step. Our job is to let ourselves be gradually dazzled. Our job is to trust that more will be revealed.

"The work is within us," Linsey always says. The truth is in us already, and a part of us knows what needs to happen. When we submit to the work, we are led out into the spacious place, even if we can't see the way.

No matter where you are today, I believe the work is within you. I believe in your capacity to step into that work and live. We must all meet on the common road of needing-God-in-our-humanity. If we could see the answer from here, we wouldn't need courage. We wouldn't need God. We wouldn't need each other. We wouldn't need faith.

Faith says, I will let myself be led by a power that is higher than I am, by someone who can see what I can't see from here.

Sometimes all we've been given is a match when what we were hoping for and waiting for was high beams. But if we'll commit to what's right in front of us, we can make the long journey with just a little light at a time.

People always ask me if I regret going to Bahrain, if it was all just too much.

"No, not for a second," I always say. We purposefully threw our lives into total upheaval, some of which we're still recovering from. But would I change the opportunity to strike out into the world and deeper into the labyrinth of my own story? No, not for a second.

In my soul, there is a gypsy, a wild and free version of myself who needs far less control, far less absolutes. I'm going to honor her by wandering a bit more than I'm comfortable with. Even if that means I have to breathe into a paper bag now and then.

Maybe she can even help me learn the dance. Yes, and amen.

24

believing your body

> When I am gentle with myself, I become gentle with others. It is this gentleness and caring, not impatience and criticism, which brings about continued growth and healing.
> —Emotions Anonymous

My hair began falling out, another postpartum treat, when we were driving from San Diego to Lake Tahoe. Luke and Lane, three-month-olds, rode in the backseat along with a breast pump plugged into the cigarette lighter.

For the entire eleven-hour drive, I obsessively combed my hands through my hair, producing alarming amounts of broken-off blonde.

The car was charged with the smell of breast milk and Flamin' Hot Cheetos, and my black yoga pants looked like I had been holding an alpaca on my lap for hours. When I got out of the car at Ikeda's, our ritual stop-off in Auburn, hair was literally hanging from the ceiling of the car. Strands of stalactites and stalagmites. Like a horror film hopped up on hormones.

Back then, I had practically no ability to step back and think about what I needed, how to feel better, what might help me experience a bit of space. Self-care didn't even register as an option. After all, I was a new mother.

Many of us realized, when it was time to take care of another human being, we didn't actually know how to take care of ourselves. And in the context of taking care of others, we had to do the hard work of both learning how to meet their needs as we were becoming sensitized to and compassionate to our own.

Many of us got the message somewhere along the way that putting our own needs and care first is an act of selfishness. I've come to see it exactly opposite. My capacity to nurture and nourish the people I love the most comes out of the overflow of my own health and well-being. A refusal to put on my own oxygen mask first isn't sacrificial, it's sabotage. None of my relationships function as they were meant to unless I am willing to first practice revolutionary self-compassion and self-care.

I look back at myself in the car on the way to Tahoe, relentlessly and obsessively combing my fingers through my hair, giving Steve the silent treatment for ordering me the wrong food at Ikeda's. I wish I could whisper in her ear: *Leeana, you are terrified and exhausted. I'm going to get you some help. I'm going to take good care of you. I love you.*

Instead, I ran my fingers through my hair. Over and over again. Paralyzed with panic. All I could do was lock horns with myself, aggressively butting up against myself when I was at my most vulnerable. This same behavior happened again when we moved to Bahrain. When I needed the greatest amount of compassion and understanding for myself, all I could summon was a sense of personal inadequacy.

Now, through all of those huge and haunting and hollow feelings, I am learning to do things much differently. I'm learning to listen to myself much more closely—with a compassionate ear—and I'm writing a new story. This story is about turning toward myself so I have the capacity to be connected intimately to the people I love. This story is about accepting my humanity, my neediness, and caring for myself immediately and tenderly.

These days, I try to pay a lot of attention to how tired I am. The fatigue triggers me in all kinds of ways. I try to be really honest with myself about the exhaustion level I feel and I force myself to make decisions accordingly. I can't mess around with this. If I allow myself to run depleted for too long, I will make decisions I regret with my kids, I will say things I don't mean to my husband, and I will suffer emotionally and mentally more than I have to. Mainly because I just don't have the resources available to deal with my life effectively.

When I'm too tired, I feel despairing. I feel like I will always feel depleted, feel slow, feel old, feel rickety.

When we returned from Bahrain, the reentry, the reverse culture shock, the reorganization, the new rhythm—all were as taxing as I assumed they'd be. You can prepare for a transition of this magnitude, even tell yourself that it's going to be demanding, but you have to actually go through it and manage yourself and your health in the process.

Life feels clumsy and inordinately complicated at first. How will we do all the things we were doing there, here?

How will we start our lives again? Preschool. Babysitters. Haircuts. Groceries. New rhythms.

The temptation, of course, is to believe things will always feel this cumbersome, this awkward, this unclear. Life will always require the amount of energy it requires right now. Things will always be this Hard. This tiring.

Mental stress catches up with us in all sorts of ways.

A few days ago, I was with my family at a restaurant. I was ordering at the counter while Steve got the kids settled at the table. I was trying to think through the order, yell at Steve to get the kids some lemonade, answer the woman's questions at the cash register, and when it was time to pay, my brain had become so completely tangled that I pulled a pack of wipes from my purse, opened up the plastic lid, pulled out a wipe, and handed it to her.

She reached out her hand with this very strange look on her face and then—ALL OF A SUDDEN—I was like, "Oh my gosh, I'm so sorry. Obviously you don't take wipes here. Oh my gosh. I'm nuts. I'm so sorry. Uhhhhh [digging around in my purse for my wallet], see, I thought I had pulled out my wallet and I was handing you my credit card. But I wasn't. I was handing you a wipe. Oh my gosh. I'm so sorry."

This is what I do lately.

Let me offer you another example from a recent trip I took to Marshalls.

Lady in Marshalls: Is that your minivan in the first spot outside?

Me: Yes.

Lady in Marshalls: Did you mean to leave all the doors open?

Me: No. No, I did not.

To borrow a line or two from Sue Monk Kidd, "The body knows things a long time before the mind catches up to them. I was wondering what my body knew that I didn't."[1]

See, when you comb your hands through your hair for eleven hours straight, when you begin leaving your car doors open in public parking lots, or you begin paying for your lunch with wipes, you need to stop and ask yourself, "Am I going crazy?"

And here's the honest truth: The answer might be, invariably, "Yes." But that's OK. Because, after all, when we pay attention to these moments of total insanity, we realize the truth. We see our bodies are telling us something our feelings can't. Our brain is signaling we are overwhelmed. Somehow. Some way. Whether it's reasonable or not doesn't matter. Whether we can identify a valid reason for our insanity or not doesn't matter.

Our physiology is telling us, *You need a break. Overload. You've hit your critical line. You've got to let go and breathe, for crying out loud!*

I, for the safety of my children and the preservation of my marriage, have started to pay more attention to these episodes. What about my life is not working for my brain? What is my body trying to tell me?

I can keep pushing, pushing, pushing, pushing (you know the drill) or I can actually listen to the smoke signal my body is giving me. I can say, "Well, I don't have as much on my plate as *her over there* and she seems to be doing fine" or "I can't really think of a reason why my brain would be overwhelmed" or "I'm not really all *that* busy." I can explain it all away. I can decide none of it's reasonable or valid. I can believe the lie that because my circumstances aren't as challenging as someone else's, I am not allowed to struggle.

Or, I can step back and say, "Hey, self, you just tried to pay for lunch with a wipe. Last week you left all the car doors open on a shopping trip. Before that you put the coffeepot (containing hot coffee) away in the cabinet with the mugs. Before that you threw all the dirty laundry into the recycling bin and your four-year-old had to bring to your attention that all her underwear were with the Diet Coke cans. Hmmmm. Let's think. What could this mean? What could this mean?"

I'm just spitballing here, but perhaps this means my brain is working overtime to process all that is going on my life, my soul, my body, my house, my surroundings. Perhaps re-entry is difficult. Maybe. Just maybe there's a strain on my physiology that I can't control. It doesn't mean I'm weak. It doesn't mean I'm flawed. It just means I'm a human being with an autonomic nervous system. Welcome to the party.

Yesterday, I put Elle in the top seat of the grocery cart, put my purse in the bottom of the cart, and instinctively began rooting around in my purse to get out my military ID. In Bahrain, we had to show our ID before coming into the grocery store on base. Without thinking, I was doing what I had done for the last two years. I was reaching for my ID. Then I snapped to. *No, I'm not in Bahrain. I'm in San Diego. In the Vons parking lot. I don't need my ID. No one is standing at the door checking IDs.*

And then last night I had a dream we were visiting Bahrain for three days. We were only there for THREE DAYS. In my dream, I was in some kind of dormitory desperately looking for my friend Jean to tell her we were there, visiting, but ONLY FOR THREE DAYS, and I couldn't find her. The dream felt like I was a lost little mouse nervously working my way through an unresolvable maze. I never found Jean.

So, even though, at this writing, we have been back in San Diego for months, I am still—clearly—getting my bearings. And, here's the real kicker, even if I *feel* like I have my bearings, my physiology may still be getting its bearings. So it doesn't really matter how I might *think* I'm doing. My body will tell me how it's really going. My subconscious will tell me how it's really going.

And if I continue to push myself, if I prod myself, if I pretend none of this matters, I will hurt myself. Studies show I can do long-term damage to my adrenal system. I can create chronic fatigue. I can shortcut my own resiliency. I can, in an attempt to get on with things and to be "strong," end up exhausting myself to the point where I lose my ability to be present in my own life. In a word, I can actually end up contributing to my own depression.

If you've been doing this, if you, in the name of "being strong" or "coping" or "getting through," have not allowed yourself the rest and recovery time you need, especially in the midst of and following a huge life transition, then now is the time to do something different. Now is *not* the time to punish yourself. Now is *not* the time to consider yourself a failure.

Now is the time to care for yourself as you would a dear friend. Now is the time to nurture yourself like a mother would a child. Now is the time for compassion, empathy, love.

Here's what will happen if you don't. You will be sleepwalking. You will be numb. You will be glassy eyed. You will be sad. I hate to say this, but you may be all those things anyway for a time. But, if you will care for yourself while you are in that state, then you stand a chance to recover; you stand a chance to be alive and awake in the world again.

And if you don't let yourself recover, you will be like so many of us who have made the fatal decision to trade in real living for the lie someone told us along the way—that in order to be really alive, we have to push ourselves until we are almost dead.

I've fallen for it a million times. And I'll fall for it again. I can absolutely assure you of that. I'll get it wrong. I'll choose the path that leads to soul death. But, and this is a big but, I know the truth now. I know the truth that will set me free. And I have the tools, now, to gently and lovingly remind myself there is a better way, a way that leads to life and life more abundant. And I'll stop and ask God to show me the way back out of the maze and into the spacious place.

Someone said to me recently, "I think there's more. I think our souls know there's more. We don't have to live like everyone's telling us we have to. There's more. And we want that more."

Yes. Yes. Yes. And the only way I know how to move toward that more is to start by being gracious with myself. There is absolutely no way I will punish myself, shame myself, push myself into more. No way.

God, lead me into your MORE, your green pasture, your consolation. Even as I am walking through the valley, even as I am paying for lunch with wipes, even as I am certified crazy, I do not have to fear. You are with me. Even when I am in the unavoidable valley, I can find breathing room. I can look into your eyes, and you will show me how to live.

25

letting go

God has come to help his people.
—Luke 7:16 NIV

Luke and Lane were big for twins. Lane was 7 pounds, 10 ounces, and Luke was 7 pounds, 7 ounces. Steve attributed their size and health to the fact that I come from sturdy stock. "You're all rawhide and rebar, Babe," he always tells me.

At one point in their pregnancy I had gained eighteen pounds in three weeks. "Could that be right?" the nurse said incredulously as he looked down at the number on the scale and back up at me. "Yep," I said shortly, far less impressed than he was. "That's right."

Toward the end, my belly was *so* big, I could rest a venti Starbucks cup on it with no problem. In fact, it was so big that people looked at me with a mix of compassion and horror. "It's sticking out so far, it looks like it could just break right off," one woman said to me in the grocery store.

I'm not sure how people expect a woman to respond to these kinds of things.

Luke and Lane were born on December 23, and in the days leading up to their birth, I was still scurrying around trying to finish last-minute Christmas shopping, great with child(ren).

I returned to my car at the Mission Valley Target, and a car had pulled into the spot next to mine so closely that I could not—no matter how many different directions I maneuvered—squeeze my substantial self into the gap between my car and theirs.

A few weeks previously the same situation had happened, and I was able to open the back of the car and crawl through the entire length of our vehicle into the driver's seat. But those days were long gone. My only option was to wait until a seemingly kindhearted stranger crossed my path and ask her if she would be willing to help me out of a tight spot.

Such a woman presented herself, and I handed over my keys to someone I had not known five seconds earlier, and asked her if she would mind terribly pulling out my car. "Well, isn't this what Christmas is all about?" she said to me through such deeply empathetic eyes that I knew I must have actually looked even more rotund than the world's fattest Santa stuffed with two oversized elves.

Days later, I went to the hospital for my routine non-stress test and the nurse announced that "Baby A's" amniotic fluid was ever-so-slightly low, so she called the OB for a consult.

"How far along are you?!?" the OB asks me (as if to say, "You look like you're sixty-two weeks pregnant!").

"Thirty-eight weeks and four days," I said.

"You've carried these babies long enough. We'll deliver them today."

I was wheeled into an operating room with equipment and medical staff everywhere. The room was quiet and focused with specialists standing by. Hushed, with a kind of looming intensity.

Luke was delivered first and then, one minute later, Lane. The doctor yelled out to me, "They're the size of singletons!" with great enthusiasm.

Within minutes we had two babies screaming at us, swaddled together in the same blanket, in Steve's arms, the mood in the room swinging dramatically. Nurses who had been serious and all-business were now laughing and posing the babies for pictures. Almost like no one knew exactly what we would find when those babies were delivered. And then the sense that everything was just fine. Absolutely just fine.

I couldn't hear or see where they took the babies to be weighed and measured, and so at some point, it occurred to me I didn't know how much they weighed.

We were all a little shell-shocked after Tina delivered her baby boy at twenty-six weeks. One pound, fourteen ounces. Eighty days in the NICU. A true miracle, and also a gnarly fight. For the final two trimesters of my pregnancy, I had been holding my breath, afraid we would probably be doing NICU time too.

When Steve told me their weights, I felt like, at that moment, everything was going to be OK. We had officially crossed the finish line of the marathon we had been running. Of course, what I didn't realize totally was that the marathon was only just beginning.

From my earliest experiences with Luke and Lane, I was fighting for them. Fighting to keep them inside as long as I possibly could. Fighting to give them breast milk, even though it was hard. Fighting for them to feel as nurtured and as loved and as safe as two babies could possibly feel.

I was desperately ferocious, crazy with love, and very often, if not always, over-caffeinated. A part of me, very deep down, knew I was actually the luckiest person on earth and all that good fortune was almost too much to bear. Like love and fear now coexisted inside me, and I couldn't tell them apart.

This is the story that describes perfectly the ferocity I felt:

Rizpah was a concubine of King Saul in the Old Testament Scriptures and the mother of his two sons, Armoni and Mephibosheth.[1] As a result of King Saul's war crimes, Rizpah's sons are hanged and denied a proper Jewish burial.

Rizpah climbs the hill where her boys' bodies are hanging and she camps out there for five months, protecting their bodies from birds and beasts of prey, holding vigil until someone buries them honorably.

I am in love with this story. It's so grisly. Like Poe. The grisliness is only overshadowed by the ferocity of Rizpah to protect and dignify the memory of her children. This is the mother I relate to, and it's almost funny to me now. How intense things have been internally. How savage these emotions. Rizpah's name means "coal" or "hot stone." I have felt that too: a white heat inside of me.

Elle's birth, three years later, ushered in something softer. Something truly different.

I was scheduled to deliver at Bahrain Specialist Hospital. One week overdue, contractions started and we were admitted to the hospital only to labor for hours upon hours with very slow-going results. Miserably slow.

At eight centimeters my labor stalled, and the doctor said it was time to go downstairs for the C-section. Hospital procedure mandated I be put fully under for the delivery, which meant neither Steve nor I would be present when our baby girl was born.

I woke up from the anesthesia to my beautiful Filipina doctor rubbing my shoulder, her emerald green scrubs and her black hair the first things I remember seeing. "We made the right decision. We made the right decision," she kept saying. "The baby was very big—4.77 kilos. We made the right decision."

The next thing I remember is Steve coming in and showing me pictures of the baby on his phone. As soon as they brought her out of delivery, he went with her to be cleaned up and weighed and measured. I didn't wake up until she was about three hours old, and by that time, she was already upstairs, so I still hadn't held her.

Steve slid pictures across his phone and I started sobbing. Like loud, uncontrolled, gutted sobs. She was so big and pink and beautiful. And he just let me lay there and sob while he flicked through the pictures again and again.

When I miscarried, I felt something was silenced deep inside me, like a mute button had been pushed. The loss and the grief and the shock taking away any kind of words. After Elle was born, I found myself silenced again. Like Someone had turned down my ability to explain it all and had turned up my ability to just experience it.

I have snapshots of Indian, Sri Lankan, Filipina, and Bahraini women floating in and around us all, caring for us, comforting us, giving us a strong start with baby Elle. I can see the huge arrow taped to my hospital room wall, directly in front of my bed, pointing us toward Mecca should we want to do our prayers. I can see the prayer rug rolled up in the bedside table, like a Gideon Bible in a hotel room. I can see her isolette parked at the foot of my bed as we looked at her for the longest time, deciding on her name. I can see Luke and Lane—just three—holding on to her as she screamed.

Through language barriers and cultural differences we brought a child into the world, who, incidentally, looked so big and so white in that hospital nursery surrounded by tiny little black-haired Bahraini babies. "I wonder which one's ours," Steve said when we went into the nursery together. We laughed when we saw her weight doubled most of the other babies.

Elle's birth was a strange sort of baptism. When I went into the water, I was terrified and exhausted and panicked and all edges. When I came up out of the water, I was softer somehow. I could no longer find the will inside myself to pinch and squeeze so intensely. I just felt the relieving release of letting go. I was far away—in another world—holding my gorgeous new girl and something broke loose.

I saw what we had been through as a family, what we were in the midst of, and I could—suddenly—see myself with such great compassion. There was so little I could actually control. The one thing I could control was how I treated myself. *Look at these beautiful children. Look at your loving husband. Look at what you've come through. Let go, Leeana, let go. Breathe. It's all going to be OK.*

Right after Luke and Lane were born, I would hear God saying to me, "I see you." This provided immense comfort in those days when everything was such a white-hot intensity. At some point, those words dissolved into "I love you." Perhaps this voice was an echo of my own. My story is the journey of first being willing to really see myself. Then, over time, learning to love what I saw. This unlocks the door and we are willing to let God love us too.

We so often project our own feelings toward ourselves onto God, assuming he thinks of us only and always in the ways we think of ourselves. Can we believe God sees us, right where we are today, no matter what we're going through? In the midst of our ferocity and intensity, can we begin to believe he loves us?

At church recently, my pastor told the story of a little girl who had been born with a cleft palate. When her classmates asked her what happened to her face, she would tell them she fell down and cut it on glass because it seemed so much more tolerable to have had an accident than to have been born "this way."

Her second-grade teacher, Miss Leonard, was everyone's favorite teacher. Each year, when it was time for the kids to have their hearing tested, Miss Leonard would stand on one side of the door and whisper something to the child who was standing with their ear to the other side of the door. The children would then repeat what Miss Leonard said to them: "You have new shoes." Or "Your shirt is green." When it was the little girl with the cleft palate's turn for her whisper test, she put her ear to the door and she heard Miss Leonard whisper to her, "I wish you were my little girl."[2]

This is our story. We come to the door with our maladies and brokenness only to be received with revolutionary love. We come to the door with our jumbled-up fear and love and our ferocious intensity, and we are met with grace. We come to the door, and we realize Christ was there knocking, all along.

For the longest time, I only heard God say, "I see you." And I would take that as such great comfort. Now, I hear him say, "I love you." And I take that as such great healing.

I have held onto the words of Anne Morrow Lindbergh: "Each cycle of a relationship is valid."[3] I have tried to trust that sometimes the "seeing" has to happen before we can internalize the "loving." Sometimes the ferocity and fear have to happen because they serve as an invitation for us to investigate the deeper waters of our stories.

And it's all OK. It's all valid. In fact, it's all grace.

Is it possible that God is the Rizpah in this story, keeping vigil for me as I have struggled? Is it possible that the Come Apart was allowed, in his grace, so that I might experience a deep, true healing?

I am finally feeling like someone has released the valve and let out some of the air in the blood pressure cuff that has been squeezing my soul. I know, now, I can hold onto the ferocious love, but I can slowly, through God's grace, let go of the fear. It's OK to exhale. That's the only way I can get the breath back. That's how I find my way back to breathing room.

The amazing thing about life's Come Aparts is that if we'll let go and do our best to keep our eyes open, we just might emerge a truer version of ourselves.

The opposite of holding our breath isn't inhaling. It's letting go.

26

watching the gutter

Lost, all lost in wonder at the God thou art.
—Saint Thomas Aquinas

I began working with a therapist who has helped me understand why all this intensity and anxiousness arrived in me in the first place. She has helped me see the connection between my young self and my now self, the old stories, my projections of my own experiences onto my children, the way my brain has held onto all the Hard and needs some help flushing it all out.

Some of us have been through events that got stuck in our bodies. When we go through things that feel like those events—in any way, shape, or form—we're triggered all over again. Our brain says something like, *Hey, this feels like it did back then. I'm scared. I'm anxious. I have no control.*

Every time she and I talk, it's like a little bit of the discomfort is diffused, and I'm able to participate in life without it all requiring so much effort to manage. I'm able to feel and experience and internalize the good more and more deeply.

I am able to forgive myself more. I am able to make peace with myself more. I am able to put my arms around myself and, genuinely, say things like, "You're doing it. What you're trying to accomplish in a day isn't easy. But you're doing great. It's OK. Breathe."

The very first step, though, was deciding I wasn't going to drift out to sea. I was going to fight to be a person who comes up and out of the water. To do that, I had to learn how to come around the table and sit next to myself instead of sending wary looks from across the divide.

I believe if we can make the all-important decision to find compassion for ourselves, to companion ourselves, we will be able to get some real work done. We will be able to let help in. We will want to get some relief for ourselves.

At some point, things will start to come back together. The feeling of being a burn victim will go away. Very slowly. The scald will settle down. We will realize we are beginning a New Way, the way of the soul. Where we were once feeling very uncomfortable in our own skin, we are now experiencing a bit of breathing room.

We are no longer locked in self vs. self. We are no longer holding our breath, ignoring our critical line.

We kept our eyes open through the Come Apart, and because of our desire to trust and participate in the transformational work of Christ, we are emerging. And we are emerging truer.

We'll be able to create and dream. We'll be able to go outside and push our kids on the swings without it feeling like running a marathon. We'll be able to make nourishing food for ourselves without it feeling like it's our job. We'll be able to ingest various soul medicines with joy instead of desperation. We'll be able to have a difficult conversation without it feeling like we lost a part of ourselves to have it. We'll be able to get up off the floor. We'll be able to laugh, laugh, laugh.

It will be hard for us to trust, though, that there isn't another Come Apart looming. We can't usually control when the Hard thing is going to arrive, so we will learn to enjoy what's in front of us. The meal. The silence. The game. The wind. The Americano. All while we can, while it lasts. While we are feeling and tasting and seeing.

We are living the words of the Beatitudes. We are blessed when we get our inside world—our mind and heart—put right. Then we can see God in the outside world. Our minds and hearts have been through an awakening, a healing, and this has given us new vision for the outside world.

The outside world is no longer working against us; we see that it has been put here for us.

Luke, at age two, immediately comes to mind. We would drive by the San Diego Bay and Luke would say, "Water. Drink it." Or we would sit out in the front yard at dusk and he would say, "Moon. Hold it." Or we would lay on our backs in the grass at the park and he'd look up at the sky and stretch his little arms toward the bright blue above us and say, "Sky. Touch it."

Yes, baby, I say to him. *That is the whole of life, of a life after God and all his beauty. Reach out and up and take it—the world around you—into your hands, enjoying every bit of the spacious place he has invited us into. It is your playground, son.* I want to whisper in his ear, in Lane's ear, in Elle's ear, every day for the rest of their lives, *If anything is holding you back or holding you up, baby, attend to it. Today. Because there is so much love waiting for you. You have no idea. Christ longs for you to bathe in the freedom and abundance.*

One day, while we were living in Bahrain, I was overcome with beige. My eyes felt so deadened and my heart was heavy. On that particular day things felt remarkably small. I felt remarkably small. Everything was filthy from the sandstorms; no real beauty to report. The smallest voice down very deep inside me was longing.

I sat in my car and I looked out my window. My eyes fell to the gutter on the other side of the road, which was running with brown water from a carwash up the street. Brown on top of beige.

Our shame, our fear, our anxiousness, our stress, our sadness—all of these depressants can beige-out our eyes. We can't see the color anymore. Enough to make you feel like you're living inside a vacuum bag.

And then, a flash. Dancing like burlesque ladies in their fancy fuchsia, a line of the hottest hot pink bougainvillea leaves pranced right on by, riding the gutter water. Absolute waste water punctuated with a kick-line of gorgeous.

Found art. The beautiful convergence of unexpected things. The redemption of what we counted lost. Found art takes the ho-hum and says it's holy. The brazen bougainvillea flirting from the dirt. Without shame. Found art says there's always beauty in the making.

God has loved me enough to take me on a journey—deeper into the world, deeper into myself, deeper into him—and he has walked with me through a mysterious unfolding. One that

I don't always understand or agree with. And yet, looking back, I can always see a certain kind of beauty that unfolded against all odds.

I am learning, very slowly and begrudgingly, that he is making all things beautiful in its time. I just don't usually fathom what God is doing from beginning to end.

If I were the Maker, I would create art from all the pretty stuff—the exotic henna, the unique architecture, the clear seas of the Gulf waters. But the Maker chooses the gritty, the gutsy, the inglorious for his glory. I hate this, and I love it. I hate that we have to go through Hard. And yet, the Beauty is so much more magnificent when it's hard-won, so much more of a miracle when we see the Maker was in and through the scraps of our lives after all.

In the end, the art of life is often *found* more than it is manifest at first glance.

I want faith large enough to always believe that the beauty is around the next bend, and—even—here in the mess too.

I want faith large enough to bank on God and his broad grace, to find beauty, even when it seems beauty has left for good.

When we are at peace with ourselves, we are able to recapture wonder. Our participation in life involves anticipation. We can put our phones down and look up at the world, poised for amazement. We can believe beauty will arrive even if it's not here now. We can believe God will show up for us even in the midst of the discomfort.

We wake up each morning and our prayer has now become a dare: *God, blow me away. Take my breath away. Show off. I dare you! And I will try to notice. With my dimly lit human eyes, I will try to notice. I will raise my hands in thanks. I will laugh my head off with delight. I will reach toward another hurting soul. I will add to the beauty. Your beauty.*

The words of cummings come back to me, rushing along the gutter water:

> i who have died am alive again today.

Amen.

postlude

continue

Continue
To dare to love deeply
And risk everything
For the good thing
—Maya Angelou

Maya Angelou has a beautiful poem called "Continue." She wrote it as a gift on the occasion of Oprah's fiftieth birthday.

The poem is a tribute to the fine art of *continuing*. In the face of oppression. In the face of ridicule. In the face of doubt, insecurity, vulnerability, naysayers. In the face of every kind of resistance, *continue*.

In the spirit of broad grace, I'd like to gift you with this one word: *continue*.

Continue **Confessing to the Trees**
Continue **Talking Back to the Brain Vultures**
Continue **Eating Your Shadow**
Continue **Beginning Again**

Continue **Borrowing Prayers**

Continue **Sharing Real Life**

Continue **Rejecting Frantic**

Continue **Googling for Help**

Continue **Being NonGodly**

Continue **Writing Letters**

Continue **Stealing Time Like Stephen King**

Continue **Getting Life under Your Nails**

Continue **Creating a Room of One's Own**

Continue **Piercing the Membrane**

Continue **Wielding Power Tools**

Continue **Chanting**

Continue **Going to the Ganges**

Continue **Saying No to the Bad Pants**

Continue **Offering Permission**

Continue **Channeling Your Inner Navy SEAL**

Continue **Jiggling**

Continue **Practicing Plenty**

Continue **Wandering Like a Gypsy**

Continue **Believing Your Body**

Continue **Letting Go**

Continue **Watching the Gutter**

It's subversive, isn't it? An act of total rebellion. To continue when all the forces of the universe are pushing back against you.

When Hard, and Unsure, and Uphill are all hunting you down, *continue* is an uprising against those voices and forces and family members who would rather you stop, hush, be a bit more ordinary or—for the love of—normal.

Everything will tell you to leave it up to the skinny people, the pretty people, the rich people, the godly people, the white men, the educated people, all the others who are more capable, qualified, and well-dressed. To boil it all down, the whispers in your ear, the screams in your head, will tell you to leave it all up to the women in the Anthropologie catalog and the rich men and Oprah. But we don't have that kind of time. We can't waste this day. We must be brazen. We must *continue*.

Wherever you are when you put this book down, whatever you are going through, I will leave you with this one, tide-changing, audacious word.

Continue.

Show up and participate in what life has in front of you, in what God is doing in your life. Continue to lean in. Continue to open your eyes. Continue to scout the beauty. Continue to create. Continue to love. Continue to get well. Continue to breathe.

And, as always, I believe in you.

recommended reading

Alcoholics Anonymous: The Big Book, 4th ed. Alcoholics Anonymous World Services, Inc., 2001.

Benner, David. *The Gift of Being Yourself: The Sacred Call to Self-Discovery*. Downers Grove: InterVarsity, 2004.

Bradshaw, John. *Healing the Shame that Binds You*. Deerfield Beach: Health Communications, Inc., 1988.

Brown, Brene. *The Gifts of Imperfection: Let Go of Who You Think You're Supposed to Be and Embrace Who You Are*. Center City: Hazelden, 2010.

Dayton, Tian. *Emotional Sobriety: From Relationship Trauma to Resilience and Balance*. Deerfield Beach: Health Communications, Inc., 2007.

Emotions Anonymous. St. Paul: Emotions Anonymous International Services, 1978.

Ford, Debbie. *The Dark Side of the Light Chasers: Reclaiming Your Power, Creativity, Brilliance, and Dreams*. New York: Riverhead, 1998.

Kidd, Sue Monk. *When the Heart Waits: Spiritual Direction for Life's Sacred Questions*. San Francisco: Harper & Row, 1990.

Lamott, Anne. *Traveling Mercies: Some Thoughts on Faith.* New York: Anchor Books, 1999.

Lewis, C. S. *A Grief Observed.* New York: HarperCollins, 1961.

Manning, Brennan. *Abba's Child: The Cry of the Heart for Intimate Belonging.* Colorado Springs: NavPress, 2002.

————. *All Is Grace: A Ragamuffin Memoir.* Colorado Springs: David C. Cook, 2011.

Norris, Kathleen. *Acedia and Me: A Marriage, Monks, and a Writer's Life.* New York: Riverhead, 2008.

Pressfield, Steven. *Do the Work!: Overcome Resistance and Get Out of Your Own Way.* Do You Zoom, Inc., 2011.

————. *The War of Art: Break Through the Blocks and Win Your Inner Creative Battles.* New York: Black Irish Entertainment, 2002.

Rohr, Richard. *Breathing Under Water: Spirituality and the Twelve Steps.* Cincinnati: St. Anthony Messenger Press, 2011.

Taylor, Barbara Brown. *Learning to Walk in the Dark.* New York: HarperOne, 2014.

Today by Emotions Anonymous. St. Paul: Emotions Anonymous International Services.

www.EmotionsAnonymous.org

acknowledgments

I can no other answer make but thanks,
And thanks, and ever thanks.
——William Shakespeare

My agent, Christopher Ferebee, remained hopeful, loyal, and enthusiastic throughout the extended evolution of this book. I feel deeply grateful for his belief in me and in this project.

The first phone call I had with my editor, Andrea Doering, was on the balcony of a hotel where we were living while we transitioned home from Bahrain. I knew, in that conversation, she got me and she got this book. And every single conversation we've had since confirms my initial impression. She has been a generous supporter and a wise counselor. I am so truly honored she took a chance on *Breathing Room*.

I will always be indebted to Angela Scheff for giving me a start.

A handful of extraordinary women read early drafts of this book—in various and chaotic stages—and helped nudge me toward clarity, truth, and my own story. They are Elaine Hamilton, Corrie Klekowski, Elyse Miller, Jamie Rettig, Tina Rose, and Linsey Wildey.

The go-getters and love-spreaders at Revell have been nothing short of all-stars. They have all been so very, very good to me. I have especially appreciated Erin Bartels, Twila Bennett, Barb Barnes, Robin Barnett, and Michele Misiak.

Wendy Johnson has been a wealth of ideas and a trusted partner.

Timely conversations with my sister, Laura Hatfield, helped to solidify content at critical junctures in my writing process.

I am so thankful for our family who continues to be on my team: Eddy and Becky Miller, Melinda Miller, Joan and Bill Tankersley, Laura, Lance, Lindsay, and Jackson Hatfield, Trey, Elyse, Nathan, Lea, and Bennett Miller, Peter, Jacquline, Fynn, and Oliver Tankersley.

I am also blessed by our church family, Flood, a community of wounded healers who reach and serve and believe.

My mom, Melinda Miller, offered details about my grandmother's life that enriched the chapter where her story is told. I'm grateful for those details and also the permission and encouragement to tell her story.

Many people allowed me to tell their stories as they intersected with my own. I so value their courage and support, especially Jean Gibbons, Rickelle Hicks, and Heather Land.

I have been challenged and changed by the truths of 12-step. This book (not to mention *me*) benefited greatly from the wisdom, tradition, and practices of Emotions Anonymous.

A handful of faithful readers keep visiting my blog and have done so all these years. I'm inspired by these people who are leaning in and showing up with such great vulnerability and courage.

Could a girl be luckier to call these women friends and warrior sisters? They have been the hands and feet of Jesus to me, walking, talking, breathing, crying, living, sharing, asking, praying, and caring every single step of the way: Debbie Cressey, Elaine Hamilton, Kate Kopp Jackson, Kara Jung, Corrie Klekowski, Tatum Lehman, Wanida Maertz, Jamie Rettig, Tina Rose, Erica Ruse, Joanna Wasmuth, and Linsey Wildey.

Two women, in particular, have been guides to me during the last year. Elaine Hamilton and Beth Slevcove injected truth and wisdom where I was only experiencing chaos. They have helped me untangle the knots, which has saved me, and which has added great richness to the material in this book.

I am thankful for Katie Gardner Sykes: her general knowledge, her specific areas of expertise, and everything in between. She is a dear friend and a deep soul.

Luke, Lane, and Elle were entertained, loved on, and played with during the mornings when I was at my desk writing. I am so indebted to Britt Pepper, Katie Slovick, and Marnie Stitzer for taking such precious care of my kids so I could write this book.

Since I've mentioned those three Tiny Tanks, I'll continue with an unapologetic confession of love for Luke, Lane, and Elle. They are extraordinary little people and the loves of my life. It is an honor to be a part of their stories.

My husband Steve makes it possible for me to write, plain and simple. He is my dearest friend and lead blocker. Without his tangible and intangible support, I would not have the space to do this work. In that way, this book is as much his as it is mine. He is passionate, intense, fierce, and tender, and I am so very grateful for our partnership, teamwork, and love story.

notes

Chapter 1 Confessing to the Trees

1. Henri Nouwen, *The Inner Voice of Love: A Journey through Anguish to Freedom* (New York: Image Books, 1999), 3.

Chapter 2 Talking Back to the Brain Vultures

1. Dr. Seuss, *Oh, The Places You'll Go!* (New York: Random House, 1960), 33.

Chapter 3 Eating Your Shadow

1. Brennan Manning, *Abba's Child: The Cry of the Heart for Intimate Belonging* (Colorado Springs: NavPress, 2002), 44.
2. See Jeremiah 2:25.
3. Brennan Manning, *Ragamuffin Gospel* (Sisters, OR: Multnomah, 1990, 2000), 26.

Chapter 5 Borrowing Prayers

1. Carrie Fountain, "Summer Practice" in *Burn Lake* (New York: Penguin, 2010), 34.
2. E. E. Cummings, "i thank You God for most this amazing," *100 Selected Poems* (New York: Grove Press, 1954), 114.
3. Ecclesiastes 3:11 NIV.
4. Nichole Nordeman, "Small Enough," Sparrow Records, 2000.
5. Rascal Flatts, "Bless the Broken Road," Lyric Street, 2008.
6. Carrie Underwood, "Jesus, Take the Wheel," Arista, 2005.

Chapter 6 Sharing Real Life

1. Psalm 68:6 Message.

Chapter 7 Rejecting Frantic

1. An acronym attributed to 12-step Recovery.

Chapter 9 Being NonGodly

1. John Bradshaw, *Healing the Shame That Binds You*, rev. ed. (Deerfield Beach, FL: HCI, 2005).
2. Romans 8:2 Message.

Chapter 10 Writing Letters

1. Tian Dayton, *Emotional Sobriety: From Relationship Trauma to Resilience and Balance* (Deerfield Beach, FL: HCI, 2007), 2.

Chapter 12 Getting Life under Your Nails

1. Ecclesiastes 3:11.
2. Louisa Kamps, "Crafting Happiness," *Stepping into Wellness*, Feb. 6, 2012, http://steppingintowellness.wordpress.com/2012/02/06/crafting-happiness-by -louisa-kamps-2/.

Chapter 13 Creating a Room of One's Own

1. John Leax, "Within Infinite Purposes: On Writing and Place," in *A Syllable of Water: Twenty Writers of Faith Reflect on Their Art*, ed. Emilie Griffin (Brewster: Paraclete Press, 2008), 21.

Chapter 14 Piercing the Membrane

1. See Mark 5:34; Luke 8:48.

Chapter 15 Wielding Power Tools

1. Emily Dickinson, "After great pain, a formal feeling comes," *The Poems of Emily Dickinson*, ed. R. W. Franklin (Cambridge, MA: Belknap Press, 1998).
2. John Greenleaf Whittier, "Maud Muller," *Yale Book of American Verse*, ed. Thomas R. Lounsbury (New Haven, CT: Yale University Press, 1912).
3. Matthew 5:4 NIV.

Chapter 17 Going to the Ganges

1. Anne Lamott, *Some Assembly Required: A Journal of My Son's First Son* (New York: Riverhead, 2013), 146.

Chapter 19 Offering Permission

1. C. S. Lewis, *Till We Have Faces: A Myth Retold* (New York: Harcourt Brace & Co., 1956), 270.
2. See Matthew 16:26.

Chapter 20 Channeling Your Inner Navy SEAL

1. BUD/S: Basic Underwater Demotion/SEAL school.

Chapter 23 Wandering Like a Gypsy

1. See 2 Kings 5:1–19.
2. Emily Dickinson, "Tell all the truth, but tell it slant," *The Poems of Emily Dickinson*, ed. R. W. Franklin (Cambridge, MA: Belknap Press, 1998).

Chapter 24 Believing Your Body

1. Sue Monk Kidd, *The Secret Life of Bees* (New York: Penguin, 2002), 69.

Chapter 25 Letting Go

1. See 2 Samuel 21.
2. Mary Ann Bird, *The Whisper Test* (No publication data).
3. Anne Morrow Lindbergh, *Gift from the Sea* (New York: Pantheon, 1955), 102.

Leeana Tankersley holds English degrees from Liberty University and West Virginia University. She and her Navy SEAL husband, Steve, are currently stationed in San Diego, California, with their three children, Luke, Lane, and Elle. Leanna writes about living from the spacious place on her blog, www.leeanatankersley.com.

Connect with Leeana at

LeeanaTankersley.com

 tankersleyleeana

 lmtankersley

 lmtankersley#

Revell
a division of Baker Publishing Group
www.RevellBooks.com